A PLUME BOOK

Quizmas Carols

GORDON PAPE is the author/coauthor of many acclaimed books, including bestselling investment guides, novels, nonfiction humor, and the Quizmas series, of which this is the third book. He is the father of three and the grandfather of eight and has spent many Christmases playing Quizmas with family and friends.

DEBORAH KERBEL, Gordon's daughter, is a seasoned Quizmas player and coauthor of the original *Quizmas: Christmas Trivia Family Fun* and *Family Quizmas*, a book of classic Christmas stories and trivia for bedtime reading to young children. She has a young son and a daughter, who are already enthusiastic participants in the family Quizmas tradition.

The authors live in the Toronto area.

Quizmas Carols

Family Trivia Fun
with Classic Christmas Songs

Gordon Pape and Deborah Kerbel

A PLUME BOOK

PLUME
Published by Penguin Group
Penguin Group (USA) Inc., 375 Hudson Street, New York, New York 10014, U.S.A. • Penguin
Group (Canada), 90 Eglinton Avenue East, Suite 700, Toronto, Ontario, Canada M4P 2Y3 (a
division of Pearson Penguin Canada Inc.) • Penguin Books Ltd., 80 Strand, London WC2R 0RL,
England • Penguin Ireland, 25 St. Stephen's Green, Dublin 2, Ireland (a division of Penguin
Books Ltd.) • Penguin Group (Australia), 250 Camberwell Road, Camberwell, Victoria 3124,
Australia (a division of Pearson Australia Group Pty. Ltd.) • Penguin Books India Pvt. Ltd.,
11 Community Centre, Panchsheel Park, New Delhi – 110 017, India • Penguin Group (NZ),
67 Apollo Drive, Rosedale, North Shore 0632, New Zealand (a division of Pearson New Zealand
Ltd.) • Penguin Books (South Africa) (Pty.) Ltd., 24 Sturdee Avenue, Rosebank, Johannesburg
2196, South Africa

Penguin Books Ltd., Registered Offices: 80 Strand, London WC2R 0RL, England

Published by Plume, a member of Penguin Group (USA) Inc. This is an authorized reprint of an
edition published by Penguin Group (Canada). For information address Penguin Group (Canada),
90 Eglinton Avenue East, Suite 700, Toronto, Ontario, Canada M4P 2Y3.

First Plume Printing, October 2007
10 9 8 7 6 5 4 3 2 1

CIP data is available.
ISBN: 978-0-452-28875-1

Printed in the United States of America

Dedication

To Shirley—the wife, mom, and nana who lovingly upholds our family's Christmas traditions.

Contents

Introduction

We all love Christmas carols. They are so much a part of our holiday tradition that it's impossible to imagine a celebration without them. Christmas without carols? It would be like spring without flowers, like a birthday without a cake, like a forest without birds. Much of the joy would be gone.

Of course, we can always have too much of a good thing and carols are no exception. A radio station in Fort Myers, Florida, starts playing them twenty-four hours a day right after Thanksgiving, prompting everyone but the most ardent carol-lover to immediately turn the dial. In 2004, labour unions in Austria demanded that stores limit carols to one hour a day, saying that their incessant playing constituted "psychological terrorism" to employees. A couple of years later, Paul Clarke, a spokesman for Britain's Union of Shop, Distributive and Allied Workers, expressed a similar view in a less dramatic way when he said that listening to the same carols over and over again could create an unhealthy working environment for retail workers. "It must drive people to distraction," he was quoted as saying.

Over the centuries, carols have been banned for all kinds of reasons. During the reign of Oliver Cromwell in England, an Act of Parliament passed in 1644 outlawed all Christmas celebrations including singing, on the grounds that it was all an excuse for debauchery and drunkenness. Enforcement was so strict that soldiers in London were empowered to arrest anyone violating the ban. It wasn't until 1660, after Charles II was restored to the throne, that the Christmas prohibition was rescinded and the English people were once again permitted to freely observe the holiday and go carolling.

Cromwell's Commonwealth wasn't the only regime to outlaw carols and Christmas. Over the centuries, singing and celebrating during the season have been forbidden in many parts of the world, including France during the Revolution and the New England states under the Puritans. If this seems outlandish today, just check the TV and newspapers during the holiday season. Carol singing is under attack in schools and public places in the United States, Canada, and elsewhere for being politically incorrect and offensive to people of other religions. In some places, school Christmas concerts have become nothing more than a fond memory.

So don't take your carols for granted. They have been threatened in the past and undoubtedly will continue to be in the future. When you sing them during the Christmas season, take a moment and give thanks for your freedom to do so.

Also give some thought to the words that are coming out of your mouth. Some carols are deeply reverent and their lyrics express that spirituality in solemn and devout terms. Think of "O Holy Night," "O Little Town of Bethlehem," and "Silent Night." Others are just plain good fun, like "Jingle Bells" and "Deck the Halls." A few make absolutely no sense at all if you take a minute to think about them. What is "I Saw Three Ships" all about, really? (You'll find one surprising answer later in this book.)

The origin of the word *carol* is a matter of some dispute among scholars. Some claim it is derived from a French word, either *carole* or *caroller,* both of which refer to a circular dance. However, it seems more likely that the etymology of the word actually dates back to the Greek *choraules,* defined in the 1883 edition of *The Dictionary of Roman and Greek Antiquities* as "musicians who accompanied on the double flute the chorus of the Greek theatre, or, in general, of the singers in a concert."

The association of *carol* with dancing does not seem so far-fetched when you go far back into history. During pagan winter solstice celebrations, people sang as they danced inside circular stone rings to give thanks for the return of the sun.

In England and other parts of Europe, many of the earliest Christmas songs were not based on the nativity at all. Rather, they were *luck-visit* songs (also called *wassail* songs), which were sung by wandering groups of sometimes disreputable revellers who were looking for free handouts of food and drink. On occasion they added implied threats to their verses to ensure compliance on the part of the often frightened recipients of their musical attentions.

The use of music in religious ceremonies to mark the birth of Jesus is said by some to date all the way back to Pope Telesphorus in the second century, although that has been called into question. There is little dispute, however, over the fact that St. Francis of Assisi revolutionized the use of Christmas music in medieval Europe when he introduced choral nativity pageants to his services. Originally, the songs were in Latin but they were soon adapted to the spoken languages of the common folk.

Martin Luther is credited with making Christmas music an integral part of religious services in Northern Europe in the sixteenth century. Luther personally translated many carols into German and wrote several new ones himself, including some especially for his own family.

In England, Charles Wesley, brother of the evangelist John Wesley, is generally recognized as the first great carol writer. Wesley, who lived from 1707 to 1788, is said to have written more than sixty-five hundred hymns during his life, including such great carols as "Hark! The Herald Angels Sing." However, the golden age of carol-writing in England was the Victorian era, which gave us music that ranged from the popular "God Rest Ye Merry, Gentlemen" to the soul-stirring "Hallelujah Chorus" from Handel's *Messiah*.

The same period also represented the apex for carol-writing in the United States. There, the inspiration was often political. Some of the best-loved American carols were originally written to promote the cause of abolition or as prayers for peace at a time when the nation was being torn apart by the Civil War. Of course, not all American carols from this time have such a tormented history. "Jingle Bells," which was originally written to celebrate Thanksgiving, not Christmas, is simply a song of fun. Some of the first secular children's carols also date from this period, such as "Up on the Housetop."

That brings us to a thorny question. What exactly qualifies as a *carol*? Everyone would agree that "I Saw Mommy Kissing Santa Claus" doesn't fit, but what about "Jingle Bells" and "Up on the Housetop"? Are they *carols* or just Christmas songs?

Some experts have declared that only faith-based music can qualify as a *carol*. But that would seem to suggest that such recent additions to our Christmas repertoire as "Do You Hear What I Hear?" and "The Little Drummer Boy" are *carols*. And it would shunt such traditional favourites as "Deck the Halls" and "Here We Come A-Wassailing" to the *songs* pile where they would reside uncomfortably alongside "I Want a Hippopotamus for Christmas" and "All I Want for Christmas Is My Two Front Teeth."

We decided not to take sides in this debate. That's why we have avoided following any rigid rules in writing this book. As far as we're concerned, a *carol* is any musical composition that we sing collectively at Christmas and which has a respectable history associated with the season. A *song* is more usually sung as a solo and is often specifically associated with a single person or group (e.g., Judy Garland and

"Have Yourself a Merry Little Christmas," and Bing Crosby and "White Christmas"). But there are no hard-and-fast rules about this.

In the end, the distinction between *carol* and *song* doesn't really matter. What is important is that you and your family have a good time trying to answer the more than five hundred Quizmas trivia questions that follow, and that you enjoy and perhaps learn from the stories behind the carols that we have included in each section.

So have fun. And Merry Christmas!

Share Your
Christmas Memories

We all have our own family memories of Christmas. This is a special invitation for you to share them with others. We have created a website at www.quizmas.net where we devote a special section to memories sent to us by our readers. Some of the stories are very moving, others are humorous, others tell of unusual traditions, and a few offer some genuine surprises.

Take some time during the holiday season to visit the website. We guarantee you'll enjoy the experience. And when you have finished reading the reminiscences, send us your story—anything that you think would bring joy or fun or hope or faith to others. It may be a favourite Christmas recipe, or a childhood memory, or a life-changing Christmas event. If it is special to you, it will be special to others as well.

We'll post the best ones on the website and perhaps we can put together a book of Christmas nostalgia that the world can enjoy.

To participate, go to www.quizmas.net and use the special email Christmas Memory form that you'll find there. Or write to:

16715–12 Yonge St.
Suite 181
Newmarket, Ontario
Canada
L3X 1X4

Please try to keep your items to less than one thousand words.

Don't be shy. Christmas is about giving, and the most valuable things we can give to anyone are good memories, because when we're gone, so are they.

Playing Quizmas Carols

Your family and friends can have a lot of fun playing Quizmas Carols together. See who can get the most answers right and earn the title of Quizmas Champion.

There are three types of questions in each chapter, each with its own difficulty rating from one to three. Correct answers receive points equal to the weighting.

PUMPKIN PIES. For anyone with a basic knowledge of Christmas carols, these should be as easy as making the traditional dessert they are named after. They're worth one point each.

PLUM PUDDINGS. These questions are more challenging and you may come across some surprises, just as you might in the old-fashioned English plum pudding. They're worth two points each.

CHESTNUTS. These are hard—in fact, they'll be the toughest nuts to crack, which is why they're worth three points each if you get the right answer.

There are many ways this book can be enjoyed. Here are some suggestions.

FAMILY QUIZMAS. A few days before Christmas, take the book to your computer and select twenty-one questions, seven from each grouping. Type up question sheets and print them. On Christmas, pass out copies to all the members of the family who are old enough to play and give everyone fifteen minutes to choose their answers. Then tally the scores. Have small prizes ready for the winners.

PARTY QUIZMAS. This is a variation on Family Quizmas to be used at Christmas parties. Give guests a copy of the questions as they arrive. Tell them to complete them during the evening and turn them in when ready. Have a prize for the winner. This is a great icebreaker and we know from experience it will generate a lot of socializing among people who may not have previously met.

GROUP QUIZMAS. One person takes the book and selects questions at random. Read each question and let everyone guess and talk about it. Once the answer has been revealed, check the stories section of the chapter. If there is one that relates to the question, read it aloud.

TEAM QUIZMAS. One person, the "designated reader," divides the room into teams of from two to four players each. Each team has a piece of paper and a pencil. The reader selects fifteen questions from anywhere in the book and reads one at a time, announcing the score value at the same time. Allow one minute for the teams to confer and write their answer. The team with the highest score at the end wins.

Special note: If you expect to have several small children who will want to play, get a copy of the original *Quizmas* book, which contains questions for both grown-ups and young people.

The Earliest Carols

Christmas carols, as we understand them today, can be traced back to the thirteenth century when St. Francis of Assisi introduced the concept of Christmas music to church services in the form of nativity plays. Of course, there were hymns of thanks to God for sending Jesus Christ prior to that, such as "A Christmas Hymn" by St. Romanos, which dates back to the sixth century. But most of the earliest Christmas music was in the form of chants.

It was not until the fourteenth century that carols based on the nativity began to become popular in Western Europe. However, wassail or luck-visit songs—some of which had their origins in pagan solstice ceremonies and were far more rowdy than religious—were commonly sung during the Christmas season. One example is "Dieus soit en cheste maison" ("May God Be in This House"), which is credited to the thirteenth century French poet and troubadour Adam de la Halle. Impoverished French nobility used to send their servants to sing this tune at the homes of wealthy people as a way of avoiding the expense of providing them with food and drink on Christmas.

As the Roman Catholic Church asserted greater control over Christmas celebrations, religious carols were written to be sung during midnight mass and Christmas Day services. One of the earliest of these was "Angelus ad Virginem," which relates the story of the visit of the angel Gabriel to Mary during which he tells her she has been chosen to bear the son of God. The origin of the carol is shrouded in mystery but it appears to date from the thirteenth century. Although it may have come from France, it was extremely popular in Britain, and the great medieval poet Geoffrey Chaucer has it being sung by the clerk in *The Canterbury Tales*.

One of the most unusual of the early carols is "I Saw Three Ships," the words to which contain so many incongruities that anyone who stops and thinks about it must wonder what this song could possibly mean and where it came from. The answers may surprise you—as will, we hope, many of the other facts you are about to discover about the earliest Christmas carols.

Brainteaser Trivia

(Answers on page 214)

Pumpkin Pies

1. Which modern-day Christmas carol, also known as "The Donkey Carol," is thought to originate from a twelfth century Latin song that began with the lyrics "Orientis partibus Adventavit asinus" ("From the East the ass has come")?

   a. "The Burgundian Carol"
   b. "The Friendly Beasts"
   c. "Ding Dong! Merrily on High"
   d. "Rudolph the Red-Nosed Reindeer"

2. What major error has been identified in the lyrics of the fifteenth century carol "I Saw Three Ships"?

   a. Ships never sail in threes
   b. Ships never sail on Christmas Day
   c. Bethlehem's port doesn't open in the morning
   d. Bethlehem has no port

3. A slightly different version of "I Saw Three Ships" is known by what name?
   a. "As I Sat on a Sunny Bank"   c. "They Sailed to Bethlehem"
   b. "All the Bells on Earth did Ring"   d. "I Spied Three Ships"

4. What were the passengers on the ships improbably doing, according to the lyrics of "As I Sat on a Sunny Bank"?
   a. Dancing and singing   c. Throwing presents
   b. Whistling and singing   d. Praising God

5. Which significant British figure is reputed to have written the sixteenth century carol "How Green Grow'th the Holly"?
   a. Queen Elizabeth I   c. Christopher Marlowe
   b. William Shakespeare   d. King Henry VIII

6. What popular medieval carol is sung by the clerk in "The Miller's Tale," which is part of Geoffrey Chaucer's classic poem *The Canterbury Tales*?
   a. "Verbum supernum, prodiens"   c. "Criste, Redemptor omnium"
   b. "Veni, Redemptor gencium"   d. "Angelus ad Virginem"

7. The word *carol* is believed to have been derived from what language?
   a. Dutch   b. German   c. Greek   d. Italian

8. Some early carols sung by wandering musicians were known as what?

   a. Minstrel music

   b. Luck-visit songs

   c. Wandering hymns

   d. Beggars' carols

9. What was carolling called before it was called *carolling*?

   a. Yodelling   b. Chanting   c. Wassailing   d. Chorusing

10. One of the earliest French carols, "Ça, bergers, assemblons nous," is said to have been sung aboard whose ship on Christmas Day, 1535?

   a. Samuel de Champlain's

   b. Étienne Brûlé's

   c. Jacques Cartier's

   d. Jacques Marquette's

Plum Puddings

11. Which traditional carol that dates back to the days of the Roman Empire (according to *The Oxford Book of Carols*) was never formally published until the nineteenth century?

   a. "The First Nowell"

   b. "O Come, O Come, Emmanuel"

   c. "O Come All Ye Faithful"

   d. "O Holy Night"

12. There are several different boar's head carols, reflecting the one-time popularity of the meat at Christmas feasts. When did the wild boar become extinct in England?

    a. Seventeenth century
    b. Eighteenth century
    c. Nineteenth century
    d. Never

13. A widely known carol, originally written in Latin, probably in the twelfth century, begins with the words: "In this rounding of the year, a life is given to the world." What was the name of the carol?

    a. "Veni, Veni, Emanuel"
    b. "Verbum caro factum est: In hoc anni circulo"
    c. "Verbum Patris Hodie"
    d. "Verbum Patris Umanatur"

14. The origin of what is now called "The Coventry Carol" can be traced back to a cycle of mystery plays that were performed in the town of Coventry during the Middle Ages. What was the name of the play from which it comes?

    a. "The Pageant of the Babe"
    b. "The Pageant of the Shepherds"
    c. "The Pageant of the Shearmen and Taylors"
    d. "The Pageant of the Lamb"

15. Which sixteenth century carol that is still popular today is cited in *The New Oxford Book of Carols* as having been sung to more tunes than any other?

    a. "Joy to the World"
    b. "While Shepherds Watched Their Flocks by Night"
    c. "Good Christian Men, Rejoice"
    d. "I Saw Three Ships"

16. One of the oldest German carols, dating back to at least the fourteenth century, is still sung today in two very different versions. What is its name?

    a. "Joseph, Lieber Joseph Mien"
    b. "Wachet Auf!"
    c. "Nun Komm, der Heiden Heiland"
    d. "Ein Kindlein in der Wiegen"

17. What thirteenth century carol with the original Latin title "In Dulci Jubilo" was taught to the composer by angels, according to his autobiography?

    a. "Joy to the World"
    b. "Good Christian Men, Rejoice"
    c. "Rejoice and Be Merry"
    d. "Shepherds, Rejoice"

18. Name the Irish carol, sometimes known as "The Ennsicorthy Carol," that dates all the way back to the twelfth century.
    a. "The Cork Carol"   c. "The Galway Carol"
    b. "The Wexford Carol"   d. "The Limerick Carol"

19. *Christmasse Carolles,* the earliest printed collection of carols, was issued by Jan van Wynken de Worde in what year?
    a. 1321   b. 1421   c. 1521   d. 1621

20. The fifteenth century carol "Joseph Was an Old Man" is also well known by which other name?
    a. "The Apple Tree Carol" c. "The Peach Tree Carol"
    b. "The Fig Tree Carol"   d. "The Cherry Tree Carol"

21. Many of the earliest English carols were of the *macaronic* variety. What does this mean?
    a. They were written partly in Latin
    b. They were sung exclusively in church
    c. They were written to be performed in pageants
    d. They had no lyrics

Chestnuts

22. Name the early carol that is thought to be derived from a series of antiphons dating all the way back to the reign of Charlemagne.

    a. "O Come All Ye Faithful"
    b. "O Come, O Come, Emmanuel"
    c. "O Little Town of Bethlehem"
    d. "O Holy Night"

23. Written in the thirteenth century, "The March of the Kings" is one of the earliest known carols surviving today in its original form. In which country did this carol originate?

    a. England   b. France   c. Germany   d. Israel

24. According to William Studwell's *The Christmas Carol Reader,* the early fifteenth century's "There Is No Rose of Such Virtue" holds which distinction?

    a. It was one of the first carols to mention Mary
    b. It was one of the first carols to use English instead of Latin
    c. It was one of the first carols written for piano
    d. It was one of the first carols banned by Oliver Cromwell

25. Perhaps the earliest known Christmas song is "Jesus Refulsit Omnium" ("Jesus Light of All the Nations"). It was composed by St. Hilary of Poitiers in what century?

    a. Fourth   b. Sixth   c. Eighth   d. Tenth

26. The rose is a very common theme in early Christmas carols ("The World's Fair Rose," "I Know a Rose Tree Springing," "Lo, How a Rose E'er Blooming," etc.). What is this flower symbolic of?

    a. The divine birth   c. The Virgin Mary
    b. The Christmas star   d. The blood of Christ

27. The fourteenth century Latin chant "Angelus Ad Virginem" was adapted and translated to become "Gabriel's Message" in the nineteenth century. Which famous rock star recorded this modified medieval carol in 1987?

    a. Sting   b. Bono   c. Prince   d. Madonna

28. One of the earliest English carols is a lullaby that dates from the fourteenth century. What is its name?

    a. "Lullay, Lullay: Als I Lay on Yoolis Night"
    b. "Swete Was the Song the Virgine Soong"
    c. "Nowel Syng We Bothe Al and Som"
    d. "Nowel: Owt of Your Slepe Aryse"

29. *New Carolls for this Merry Time of Christmas,* published in 1661, is the oldest known source for an English carol that dates back to at least the 1500s. What is the carol, which is still sung and recorded today?

    a. "Rejoice and Be Merry"   c. "The Cherry Tree Carol"

    b. "A Virgin Unspotted"   d. "The Blessings of Mary"

30. Which fifteenth century English carol was inspired by a legend surrounding the relics of the Three Wise Men?

    a. "The March of the Kings"   c. "I Saw Three Ships"

    b. "Star of the East"   d. "The First Nowell"

31. According to the carol, who was aboard the vessels in "I Saw Three Ships"?

    a. Joseph and Mary   c. Mary and Jesus

    b. Joseph, Mary, and Jesus   d. No one

32. Who were the passengers on the ships according to the lyrics of "As I Sat on a Sunny Bank"?

    a. Joseph and Mary   c. Mary and Jesus

    b. Joseph, Mary, and Jesus   d. No one

33. According to the *Canadian Encyclopedia,* the earliest Canadian carol to be published was probably J.P. Clarke's "A Canadian Christmas Carol." In what year did it first appear?

    a. 1653   b. 1753   c. 1853   d. 1953

34. What traditional English carol was featured in the opening titles of the classic 1935 film version of *David Copperfield*?

    a. "I Saw Three Ships"   c. "The Coventry Carol"
    b. "The Boar's Head Carol"   d. "Here We Come A-Wassailing"

35. In the first verse of "The Boar's Head Carol," which spices are said to bedeck the head?

    a. Thyme and basil   c. Mint and oregano
    b. Bay and rosemary   d. Pepper and saffron

36. "Dieus soit en cheste maison," an old French luck-visit song, translates into English as what?

    a. "Two Saints in My House"
    b. "An Angel Sang Upon My Chest"
    c. "May God Be in This House"
    d. "The Lord Is in All Our Homes"

Did You Know?

Dining on Boar's Head

It seems gross to most people today, but for centuries feasting on boar's head at Christmas (and prior to that at solstice celebrations) was a much-anticipated annual tradition.

The ritual appears to have had its origin in Norse mythology where the god and goddess of fertility, Frevr and Freya, rode on boars named Hildisvin and Gullenbursti. Over time, it became traditional to sacrifice a boar to Freya at the time of the winter solstice. Later Christians appropriated the idea (as they did so much else from old pagan rites).

Although wild boars disappeared from England in the seventeenth century—too tasty, it seems—the tradition of the boar's head feast is observed to this day at Oxford University's The Queen's College and at Hurstpierpoint College in West Sussex. (Oglethorpe University in Atlanta, Georgia, brought the celebration to the United States.)

The events take us back centuries in time with their spectacle and pageantry. Wikipedia describes the Hurstpierpoint ceremony, which takes place on the first Wednesday in December, as follows:

The Boar's Head is carried on a platter carried by four Sacristans and preceded by the mustard pot carried by a fifth. The remainder of the Senior School lines the cloisters which form three sides of the Inner Quadrangle, the fourth being formed by the Chapel and Dining Hall. The lights are extinguished and the procession, its members carrying candles, moves from the east of the college through the cloisters lined by unusually silent students and back through the Chapel to the vestry.

At The Queen's College, the start of the colourful ceremony is announced by the blare of trumpets. The boar's head with an orange in its mouth is carried into the dining hall by four chefs on a seventeenth century silver platter accompanied by torch-bearers on either side as the choir sings the traditional carol, which begins with the words:

The boar's head in hand bear I
Bedecked with bay and rosemary
I pray you, my masters, be merry

After the procession winds through the hall, the boar's head is set before the College Provost, who presents the orange to the chief singer and distributes sprigs of bay, rosemary, and holly to the diners. Then the Provost slices the meat and all assembled tuck into what must be a very jolly meal.

The Mystic

"Good Christian Men, Rejoice" is one of our most popular carols. Children especially enjoy it because of its bright, lively tune. But what most people don't realize when they sing it at Christmastime is that it dates back some 700 years and, if we are to take the writer at his word, was taught to him by an angel!

Heinrich Seuse (more commonly known as Suso) was born into a noble family on the German side of Lake Constance near the end of the thirteenth century. He grew up to become a Dominican monk and one of the leading exponents of mysticism of his time, having studied under Johannes Eckhart, an influential and controversial figure who in later life was hauled before the Inquisition in Cologne and forced to recant some of his writings.

From what we can deduce, in his early years Seuse appears to have espoused the idea of self-flagellation and other acts of painful penance as the way to Christ. However, he eventually left this mode of thinking behind and adopted a more contemplative approach to God, which was reflected in such writings as *The Little Book of Eternal Wisdom* and *The Little Book of Truth*. At one point in his writing he describes the Supreme Being in a way that is sure to confound mathematicians: "God is a circular ring whose centre is everywhere and circumference nowhere."

If we are to take his writings literally (or at least the translation by T.F. Knox published in 1865 under the title *The Life of the Blessed H. Suso, by Himself*), Seuse communed directly with angels in both an intellectual and a physical sense. And it was from one of those encounters that the carol "Good Christian Men, Rejoice," originally titled "In Dulci Jubilo," was passed to him.

In Knox's book, Seuse is quoted as describing how angels came to him at daybreak one day, appearing as "heavenly musicians sent by God." Seuse says he was told they were sent by God to bring him "heavenly joys," whereupon they began "a joyous song about the infant Jesus." Seuse describes how he was drawn into a dance with the angels, writing: "This dance was not of the kind that are danced on earth, but it was a heavenly movement, swelling up and falling back again into wild abyss of God's hiddenness."

And thus did "Good Christian Men, Rejoice" become part of our Christmas traditions. Seuse was declared "Blessed" by Pope Gregory XVI in 1831.

Gloria in Excelsis Deo

There is a great deal of debate as to whether "Angels We Have Heard on High" is a relatively new carol (the *Oxford Book of Carols* concludes it probably dates from eighteenth century France) or one of the oldest carols in existence.

The dispute seems to stem from the carol's beautiful refrain, which uses the words "Gloria in excelsis Deo," Latin for "Glory to God in the Highest." That phrase is one of the oldest in Christianity and its use in musical form during Christmas services is said to date all the way back to the time of Pope Telesphorus, head of the Roman Catholic Church in the early second century, who is purported to have directed that it be used at evening services on Christmas. Supporters of this view claim that this was indeed the genesis of the "Angels We Have Heard on High" that we sing today, in which the word *Gloria* is extended over several bars in what is known as a melismatic sequence, which means changing the pitch of a single syllable as it is sung.

But according to *The Christmas Carol Reader* by William Studwell, the story of Telesphorus and this carol is a "myth" and "should be cast in the trash can of history." He concurs with *The New Oxford Book of Carols* that "Angels We Have Heard on High" dates from eighteenth century France.

We leave it to the scholars to debate this one, which they undoubtedly will do for centuries to come. What we do know is that "Gloria in Excelsis Deo" has now become a standard part of Christmas celebrations in several beautiful forms, including the Latin version of "O Come All Ye Faithful" ("Adeste Fideles"). If Pope Telesphorus was in any way responsible for that, his name deserves to be remembered.

They Sailed into ... Where?

Everyone loves "I Saw Three Ships." It's a rousing carol, full of rhythm and imagery. Except that a lot of that imagery is, well, bizarre!

Have you ever thought about the words to this song as you belted it out at a Christmas service? Probably not! If you had, you might have stopped in mid-stanza and muttered something like: "What the heck is this all about, anyway?"

Consider some of the lines from the song, and its virtual twin "As I Sat on a Sunny Bank."

O they sailed into Bethlehem. Into Bethlehem? A land-locked town in the middle of a semi-desert? A town that sits twenty-five hundred feet above sea level? Perhaps the reference to "sailing" is meant to be allegorical. Certainly that's the only way this makes any sense.

And what was in those ships all three? Our Saviour Christ and his lady. Three ships. Why only two people? To add to the confusion, the words in "As I Sat on a Sunny Bank" tell us that the two were "Joseph and his fair lady."

O he did whistle and she did sing. These words from "As I Sat on a Sunny Bank" convey the strange image of Joseph whistling as the ships sail past. If there is any other reference to such unusual behaviour by Joseph in Christmas tradition, we don't know about it. In an even more unorthodox but seldom heard version from the English county of Kent, it is Jesus Christ who is supposedly doing the whistling.

So how do we explain these outlandish lyrics? And what is the significance of *three* ships, which is not addressed in either version of the carol?

Surprisingly, according to *The New Oxford Book of Carols,* the ancient origin of "I Saw Three Ships" actually had nothing to do with the birth of Jesus, except by association. The story is that the ships actually contained the skulls of the Three Kings, which were being transported to their final resting place in the Cathedral of Cologne, Germany, in the twelfth century. The book cites an early English version of the carol sung by river boatmen, which makes reference to the ships containing "three crawns"—skulls to us. That gruesome picture doesn't mesh well with festive Christmas celebrations, so it's no surprise that later versions changed the lyrics to something more cheerful and more appropriate to the season.

English Carols

Many of our most beloved carols come from England, and some can be traced back all the way to medieval times. The origins of many English carols that are still popular today have been lost in the mists of time, causing even scholars who have spent years tracing their beginnings to throw up their hands in dismay.

Many of these traditional carols have a folkloric history, which means that several different versions exist depending on the region—or even the village—in which they were sung. While some of these pay homage to God and Jesus, others are luck-visit carols—songs of merriment and drinking that were often sung (discordantly, we might imagine) by revellers wandering through the town looking for handouts from wealthy landowners. Some of the words are very specific in terms of the carollers' demands, such as these verses from "The Yorkshire Wassail Song" as printed in *Eight Traditional Christmas Carols,* compiled by the famous English composer Ralph Vaughan Williams in 1919.

We've got a little purse
Made of stretching leather skin

We want a little money
To line it well within.

Call up the butler of this house,
Put on his golden ring;
Let him bring us up a glass of beer,
The better we shall sing.

So bring us out a table,
And spread it with a cloth;
And bring us out your mouldy cheese,
And then your Christmas loaf.

The reference to mouldy cheese in the last verse didn't imply that
the merry drunkards would be happy with leftovers. The reference is to
blue cheese, a great delicacy. If they got everything they demanded—
and it seems that many of those receiving their "good wishes" complied
for fear of retribution—the Christmas season must have left them
feeling very satisfied with themselves!

During the eighteenth and nineteenth centuries, carols celebrating
debauchery and drinking disappeared from the scene. The transition is
best seen in the hymns of Charles Wesley, a prolific eighteenth century
writer who is estimated to have penned some sixty-five hundred religious songs including such all-time favourites as "Hark! The Herald
Angels Sing." Like his older brother, John, Charles Wesley was a leader

of the Methodist movement, which in its early stages was a very strict doctrine that frowned on frivolity and excess. Certainly, you would never have caught a devout Methodist singing for mouldy cheese at the door of a rich merchant!

The piety of Wesley's hymns carried on through the Victorian era of the nineteenth century when religious themes such as the birth of the Saviour, the holiness of Mary, and the greatness of God permeated the lyrics of such carols as "Angels from the Realms of Glory," "As With Gladness, Men of Old," and "See, Amid the Winter's Snow."

During this period, we also find oblique references to some of the great social causes of the time, such as the injustice of slavery, embedded in the carols—for example, in James Montgomery's "Angels from the Realms of Glory."

Sadly, the art of Christmas carol composition seems to have died in England with the passing of Queen Victoria. In our research, we could not find a single popular carol of English origin dating from after 1901. It was as if the fountain was suddenly turned off and never restarted.

This chapter deals mainly with carols of English origin, although in some cases other regions of the British Isles inevitably are involved—James Montgomery, for example, was born in Ayrshire, Scotland. However, you will find most of the references to carols from Ireland, Wales, and Scotland in the Around the World section of this book.

Brainteaser Trivia

(Answers on page 215)

Pumpkin Pies

1. The melody for "What Child Is This?" is based on which traditional love song?

   a. "Greensleeves"

   b. "Barbara Allen"

   c. "The Banks of Sweet Primroses"

   d. "Betsy, the Servant-Maid"

2. What Christmas song is sometimes mistakenly called "The Portuguese Carol"?

   a. "The First Nowell"

   b. "Angels We Have Heard on High"

   c. "O Come All Ye Faithful"

   d. "Christians, Awake"

3. What animal is mentioned in the refrain of "The Holly and the Ivy"?

   a. Boar   b. Deer   c. Bear   d. Lark

4. In the version of "The Twelve Days of Christmas" that is most commonly sung today, what are there eleven of?

    a. Maids   b. Lords   c. Pipers   d. Ladies

5. What 1952 British movie has the same title as a traditional Christmas carol?

    a. "Deck the Halls"
    b. "Rejoice and Be Merry"
    c. "The Holly and the Ivy"
    d. "The Twelve Days of Christmas"

6. The inspiration for "The Twelve Days of Christmas" comes from a game that was played on which holiday?

    a. Christmas   c. Twelfth Night
    b. St. Stephen's Day   d. Candlemas

7. In "We Wish You a Merry Christmas," what are the carollers demanding?

    a. Piggy pudding   c. Veggie pudding
    b. Figgy pudding   d. Bread pudding

8. In "The Twelve Days of Christmas," what is a calling bird?

    a. A mockingbird   c. A blackbird
    b. A robin   d. A thrush

9. In verse four of "The First Nowell," in what direction is the star moving?

a. Northeast   b. Northwest   c. East   d. West

10. The lyrics of the sixteenth century carol "God Rest Ye Merry, Gentlemen" are famously cited in which renowned literary work?

a. *Twelfth Night*
b. *A Christmas Carol*
c. *A Visit from St. Nicholas*
d. *The Nutcracker and the Mouse King*

11. In the traditional carol "Christmas Hath Made an End," the phrase "well-a-day" is repeated several times. What emotion does it convey?

a. Happiness   b. Mirth   c. Sorrow   d. Love

12. What beverage is being drunk in "Wassail! Wassail All Over the Town"?

a. Meade   b. Wine   c. Brown ale   d. Whisky

13. The Twelve Days of Christmas end on what holiday?

a. Christmas   b. New Year's   c. Advent   d. Epiphany

14. Who or what is singing in "Joy to the World"?

    a. Earth and sky   c. Jesus and Mary

    b. Men and angels   d. Heaven and nature

15. The lyrics of "Joy to the World" are a paraphrase of some verses from which psalm?

    a. Psalm 23   b. Psalm 101   c. Psalm 72   d. Psalm 98

16. What sets "We Wish You a Merry Christmas" apart from most other traditional Christmas carols?

    a. It contains a reference to the New Year's celebration

    b. Its lyrics are written in the plural form

    c. It mentions dessert

    d. It's written in iambic pentameter

17. "Christians, Awake!" was originally penned by John Byrom as a Christmas gift to whom?

    a. His wife   c. John and Charles Wesley

    b. His daughter   d. His students

18. Charles Wesley, author of "Hark! The Herald Angels Sing," was a prolific composer. How many hymns is he credited with?

    a. Five hundred   c. Thirty-five hundred

    b. Fifteen hundred   d. Sixty-five hundred

19. In one version of "The Twelve Days of Christmas" that is still sung in Sussex, the four calling birds are replaced by what?

a. Canaries   b. Catbirds   c. Kingfishers   d. Kingbirds

20. What nursery rhyme was set to music by author/poet Edith Nesbitt Bland, who wrote the classic book *The Railway Children*?

a. "Christmas Is Coming"
b. "The Holly and the Ivy"
c. "We Wish You a Merry Christmas"
d. "What Child Is This?"

Plum Puddings

21. Name the carol whose tune was based on a Swedish ode to spring and was originally written for children.

a. "The Holly and the Ivy"
b. "While Shepherds Watched Their Flocks"
c. "Good King Wenceslas"
d. "Oh Come All Ye Faithful"

22. John Byrom, the author of the lyrics of "Christians, Awake!", invented a system of what?

a. Accounting   c. Fingerprinting
b. Shorthand   d. Engraving

23. What was the unusual name of the Manchester street on which John Byrom lived?

    a. Hanging Ditch   c. Dead Man's Passage

    b. Gallows Row   d. Gibbet Lane

24. *A Festival of Nine Lessons and Carols* (the Christmas carol service from King's College, Cambridge) begins each year with a boy singing as a solo the first verse of which carol?

    a. "Silent Night"   c. "Once in Royal David's City"

    b. "Ave Maria"   d. "Joy to the World"

25. *A Festival of Nine Lessons and Carols* has been an annual Christmas Eve musical event at King's College, Cambridge, since what year?

    a. 1618   b. 1718   c. 1818   d. 1918

26. The author of the lyrics for "Angels from the Realms of Glory" was twice imprisoned for what crime?

    a. Blasphemy   c. Trespassing

    b. Libel   d. Vagrancy

27. Good King Wenceslas is the patron saint of what country?

    a. Slovakia   b. Austria   c. Hungary   d. Czech Republic

28. What carol, written to the tune of an old English folk song, is now rarely sung in Britain although it is popular in the United States?

    a. "The Holly and the Ivy"   c. "What Child Is This?"

    b. "The Wassail Song"   d. "The Carol of the Bells"

29. The seldom-sung third verse of "God Rest Ye Merry, Gentlemen" tells of the shepherds leaving their flocks to go to the stable. What were the weather conditions at the time, according to the carol?

    a. "Night all still and calm"

    b. "Soft breezes stirred the grass"

    c. "Tempest, storm and wind"

    d. "The still, cold gray of dark"

30. Which age-old rivalry is symbolized in the title of the English carol "The Holly and the Ivy"?

    a. Church vs. state   c. Male vs. female

    b. Man vs. nature   d. Science vs. art

31. What carol was written by an insurance agent?

    a. "As With Gladness, Men of Old"

    b. "The First Nowell"

    c. "While Shepherds Watched Their Flocks by Night"

    d. "Christians, Awake!"

32. Each verse of "Wassail! Wassail All Over the Town" contains a toast to someone or something. Which of the following is not included in the toasts?

   a. Maids　　　b. Cattle　　　c. Horses　　　d. Sheep

33. What carol is sung every Christmas season at Oxford University's The Queen's College?

   a. "The Boar's Head Carol"
   b. "The Seven Joys of Mary"
   c. "Tomorrow Shall Be My Dancing Day"
   d. "The Cherry Tree Carol"

34. "On Christmas Night All Christians Sing" is also known by what name?

   a. "The Sussex Carol"　　　c. "The Suffolk Carol"
   b. "The Exeter Carol"　　　d. "The London Carol"

35. What are the main ingredients of wassail?

   a. Fruit juice and beer　　　c. Mead and wine
   b. Beer, wine, and spices　　　d. Beer and honey

36. Although the carol officially dates from the mid-eighteenth century, the melody for "Good King Wenceslas" actually goes back to what period?

    a. The first century
    b. The eighth century
    c. The tenth century
    d. The fourteenth century

37. In real life, Wenceslas was not a king at all, although he did hold a noble title. What was it?

    a. Prince   b. Duke   c. Baron   d. Earl

38. In "The Holly and the Ivy," with whom is holly associated?

    a. Baby Jesus   b. God   c. Joseph   d. Mary

39. "Now the Holly Bears a Berry" is a traditional English carol that is also known by what name?

    a. "The St. Joseph Carol"
    b. "The Virgin Mary Carol"
    c. "The St. Nicholas Carol"
    d. "The St. Day Carol"

40. "Wassail! Wassail All Over the Town" is also known by what name?

    a. "The Yorkshire Carol"
    b. "The Cornwall Toast"
    c. "The Warwickshire Carouse"
    d. "The Gloucestershire Wassail"

Chestnuts

41. What popular West Country carol plays an important role in Thomas Hardy's classic novel *Under the Greenwood Tree*?

    a. "Rejoice, Ye Tenants of the Earth"
    b. "Awake, and Join the Cheerful Choir"
    c. "The Holly and the Ivy"
    d. "The Boar's Head Carol"

42. The modern version of "Lo! He Comes with Clouds Descending" was first published by the Reverend Martin Madan, who is perhaps better known for a 1780 polemic titled *Thelyphthora, or a treatise on female ruin*. What controversial idea did this work advocate?

    a. Divorce   b. Prostitution   c. Polygamy   d. Abortion

43. Which U.S. university has an annual boar's head ceremony modelled after that of The Queen's College?

    a. Duke   b. Clemson   c. Oglethorpe   d. Rutgers

44. How long must a graduate of The Queen's College, Oxford, wait before being invited back to attend the annual "Boar's Head Gaudy"?

    a. Five years   c. Twenty-five years
    b. Fifteen years   d. Fifty years

45. Holly and ivy are traditional symbols for what?
    a. Good and evil   c. Fire and water
    b. Life and death   d. Summer and winter

46. Which English folk carol is divided into three narrative parts?
    a. "The Wassail Song"   c. "I Saw Three Ships"
    b. "The Cherry Tree Carol"   d. "Shepherds, Arise!"

47. When the great English composer Ralph Vaughan Williams died in 1958, he left the music for an unfinished Christmas play named after a popular carol. What was the carol?
    a. "The Twelve Days of Christmas"
    b. "The Holly and the Ivy"
    c. "The First Nowell"
    d. "Deck the Halls"

48. In Part II of "The Cherry Tree Carol," what does the angel say should be used to christen the Baby Jesus?
    a. Red wine   c. Tears of the lamb
    b. White wine   d. Spring water

49. In Part III of "The Cherry Tree Carol," with whom does Mary converse?
    a. Joseph   b. God   c. An angel   d. Jesus

50. "What Child Is This?" is the best-known carol that is sung to the tune of "Greensleeves." Name another one.

   a. "Rejoice and Be Merry"
   b. "The Old Year Now Away Is Fled"
   c. "In Those Twelve Days"
   d. "Tomorrow Shall Be My Dancing Day"

51. "God Rest Ye Merry, Gentlemen" is considered to be the quintessential English carol. However, historian A.L. Lloyd wrote that at least the first eight bars of the tune probably came to England from what European country?

   a. Germany   b. France   c. Italy   d. Spain

52. Although all of the wassail songs have the same general theme, none agree on what the cup or bowl is made of. In the best known of these carols, "Here We Come A-Wassailing," the second verse describes the wassail cup as made of what?

   a. Cedar branches   c. Mulberry boughs
   b. Chestnut root   d. The rosemary tree

53. What is the wassail bowl made of in "Wassail! Wassail All Over the Town"?

   a. Holly wood   c. Cherry wood
   b. Stout oak   d. White maple

54. There are many wassail songs. One of the more obscure is called "A Wassail, a Wassail Throughout All This Town." In this carol, what is the bowl said to be made of?

a. Serviceberry wood
b. Elderberry bough
c. Apple wood
d. Tannis root

55. What Victorian era poet wrote the lyrics to the carol "In the Bleak Mid-Winter"?

a. Elizabeth Barrett Browning
b. John Keats
c. Lord Byron
d. Christina Rossetti

56. Reginald Heber is best remembered for his hymn "Holy, Holy, Holy," but in 1811 he wrote a Christmas carol with a theme drawn from a verse in the Book of Job. What is its title?

a. "Rouse, Rouse from Your Slumbers"
b. "Brightest and Best of the Sons of Morning"
c. "Joy to the World"
d. "Rejoice, Ye Tenants of the Earth"

57. What carol with an English-language verse and a Latin refrain is thought by some scholars to have originated in Italy?

a. "The Snow Lay on the Ground"
b. "See, Amid the Winter's Snow"
c. "On Christmas Night All Christians Sing"
d. "A Virgin Unspotted"

58. During the *Oie'l Verrey* (The Eve of Mary's Feast) Christmas Eve service on the Isle of Man, the parishioners of the church would start singing after the prayers had been read. Instead of a chorus, the carollers would each sing in turn, stopping only when what happened?

a. They forgot the words   c. The morning star appeared in the sky

b. Their voices broke   d. Their candle went out

59. A poem written late in life by Christina Rossetti, who wrote the lyrics to "In the Bleak Mid-Winter," also was set to music in a carol that is seldom heard today. What is its name?

a. "See, Amid the Winter's Snow"

b. "Love Came Down at Christmas"

c. "The Angel Gabriel from God Was Sent"

d. "Let All That Are to Mirth Inclined"

60. Who wrote the lyrics of "Joy to the World?"

a. Isaac Watts   c. William Chatterdon Dix

b. Charles Wesley   d. James Montgomery

61. What carol tells the whole story of the life of Christ in its eleven verses?

a. "The Cherry Tree Carol"

b. "The Blessings of Mary"

c. "Tomorrow Shall Be My Dancing Day"

d. "On Christmas Night All Christians Sing"

Did You Know?

"The Portuguese Carol"

Everyone has been guilty of jumping to conclusions at times. The Duke of Leeds did it way back in 1795, and the mistake he made has carried down more than two centuries.

During the holiday season that year, the duke attended a special service in the chapel of the Portuguese Embassy in London, during which the organist, Samuel Webbe, performed a hymn the duke had never heard before. He was so impressed with the melody that he commissioned an arrangement that was performed at the Concerts of Ancient Music, of which he was a patron. Since he had first heard the hymn at the Portuguese Embassy, he assumed, wrongly, that it had originated in that country and the piece became known as "The Portuguese Carol."

In fact, the true origin of "Adeste Fideles," better known today as "O Come All Ye Faithful," is something of a mystery. The best guess is that the first version was written by an Englishman, John Francis Wade, in the mid-eighteenth century while he was a resident at the English College in Douai, France. But since most of the college's documents were destroyed during the French Revolution, no one can affirm this with certainty.

What we do know is that over the years "O Come All Ye Faithful" has become one of the best loved of all the carols. And it most certainly did not come from Portugal.

The Passionate Scot

"Angels from the Realms of Glory" is one of those carols that everyone loves. It is brisk, tuneful, spiritual, and, well, just fun to sing. But few people know that the lyrics were written by a firebrand Scot named James Montgomery who spent most of his life in England, where he campaigned for Ireland's freedom from British rule as well as for the abolition of slavery.

As editor of the *Sheffield Iris,* Montgomery used his public platform to rail against the evils of the world. His outspoken editorials and publishing policies twice landed him in jail for libel: once for reporting the details of a riot, and a second time for publishing a poem glorifying the fall of the Bastille. He passed his time in jail writing poems, which were later published as *Prison Amusements.* Each time he emerged more determined than ever to carry on his battles.

Despite his journalistic campaign for social justice, Montgomery has become little more than a footnote in history and would probably have been completely forgotten had he not written a poem that was later set to music by Henry Smart and became a Christmas standard.

Although few of us realize it, we echo Montgomery's passion for the rights of the underdog every time we sing the popular carol. One of the verses—which for many years was omitted from the official texts of the song—goes as follows:

Sinners, wrung with true repentance,
Doomed for guilt to endless pains,
Justice now revokes the sentence,
Mercy calls you; break your chains.

Montgomery did live to see the abolition of slavery in Britain in 1833 (he died in 1854). But it would be another century before his other great obsession, Ireland's independence, became a reality.

The Good Duke

Although the lyrics to "Good King Wenceslas" were written by an Englishman, John Mason Neale, there is nothing English about the carol's title character. He wasn't British, he never visited the country, and in fact he was not even a king. In reality, he was Duke Václav of Bohemia and is remembered not for trudging out into the snow to bring food and pine logs to a peasant (a silly idea when you think about it since we're told the man lived "right against the forest fence") but for spreading Christianity in what was at the time a largely pagan region of Central Europe.

According to the *Catholic Encyclopedia,* Václav was born in 903 (other accounts say 907), the oldest son of Duke Vratislaus I and his wife, a devout pagan who became known as Drahomíra the Arrogant. When Vratislaus I died in 921 (or 916 by some accounts), Václav succeeded to the title at the age of eighteen (or perhaps fourteen; in any event he was very young). However, instead of being raised by his pagan mother as you might expect, he was reared by his paternal grandmother, a devout Christian lady who was later canonized by the Roman Catholic and Orthodox churches as Saint Ludmila.

As a result of Ludmila's influence, Václav grew up to be a fervent believer in Christianity and used his power and influence to spread the religion throughout the area that is today the Czech Republic by building great churches and holding bountiful feasts.

Unfortunately for him, his mother (who had previously arranged to have Ludmila strangled) plotted with her younger son, Boleslaus, to get rid of Václav as well. The terrible deed was probably done in 935 (although some scholars say 929) when young Václav was "hacked to pieces" (the words of the *Catholic Encyclopedia*) at the church door in the town of Stará Boleslav.

Today, Wenceslas (officially spelled Wenceslaus by the Catholic Church) is the patron saint of the Czech Republic, and his statue in Prague's Wenceslas Square has become a major tourist attraction.

Brrrr!

There have been many depictions in carols of the conditions in Bethlehem when Christ was born, but none is anywhere near as bone-chilling as the first verse of Christina Rossetti's "In the Bleak Mid-Winter."

In the bleak mid-winter, frosty winds made moan;
Earth stood hard as iron, water like a stone;
Snow had fallen, snow on snow, snow on snow,
In the bleak mid-winter, long ago.

Franco/Germanic Carols

While many of the most popular carols we sing today originated in England, we also owe a debt of gratitude to France, Germany, and Austria, from which we received such beautiful Christmas music as "Silent Night" and "O Holy Night."

Although there are some older carols in German, it was Martin Luther who provided the real impetus for making music a part of the Christmas tradition. He personally translated several old Latin carols into German (e.g., "Nun Komm, der Heiden Heiland") and wrote others himself, such as "Vom Himmel hoch da komm ich her" ("From Heaven Above I Come to You"). However, contrary to popular belief, he did *not* write "Away in a Manger," which erroneously came to be known in America as "Luther's Cradle Hymn."

The most beloved German-language carol is, of course, "Silent Night," which has become a part of almost every Christmas celebration. The story of how it came to be written is in turn moving, humorous, and deeply spiritual. It is also somewhat controversial, as you'll read later in this chapter.

In France, the region of Provence produced many of that country's most memorable carols, including "Bring a Torch, Jeanette, Isabella" and the haunting "O Holy Night," the lyrics to which were improbably written by a wine merchant.

You'll discover many more intriguing facts about the Franco/Germanic origins of some of our greatest Christmas carols as you test your knowledge with our Quizmas questions and read the amazing stories behind the songs.

Brainteaser Trivia

(Answers on page 216)

Pumpkin Pies

1. "Silent Night" was written in the mountain town of Oberndorf, which was located in what country?

   a. Germany   b. Switzerland   c. Austria   d. Liechtenstein

2. Which carol was known for years in North America as "Luther's Cradle Hymn" but in fact has nothing to do with Martin Luther and is rarely sung in Germany?

   a. "A Child This Day Is Born"   c. "Mary Had a Baby"
   b. "Away in a Manger"   d. "Lullay, Thou Tiny Little Child"

3. In the French carol "Quittez pasteurs," what are the shepherds *not* told to leave?

   a. The hillside   b. The brook   c. Their sheep   d. The pasture

4. What is the literal English translation of "O Tannenbaum"?

   a. "O Christmas Tree"   c. "O Green Tree"
   b. "O Fir Tree"   d. "O Eternal Tree"

5. What is the French name for "O Tannenbaum"?
   a. "Arbre de vie"   c. "Arbre de Noël"
   b. "Mon beau sapin"   d. "Noël dans le forêt"

6. Who are the two girls named in the carol "Bring a Torch, Jeanette, Isabella"?
   a. Princesses   c. Milkmaids
   b. Shepherdesses   d. Friends of Mary

7. Which two countries claim authorship of "The First Nowell"?
   a. France and Germany   c. Belgium and France
   b. England and France   d. Switzerland and France

8. The French carol "Guillô, Come, and Robin Too" tells them to bring their "pipe and tabor." What kind of instrument is a tabor?
   a. A flute   b. A horn   c. A drum   d. A harp

9. "Silent Night" was originally played on which musical instrument?
   a. Organ   b. Piano   c. Spinet   d. Guitar

10. What is the French version of "Jingle Bells" called?
    a. "Clac-clac-clac"   c. "Nuit d'hiver"
    b. "Vive le vent"   d. "Boule de neige"

11. According to the lyrics, what is the Christmas tree in "O Tannenbaum" supposed to teach us to possess?
    a. Life eternal
    b. Beauty
    c. Steadfastness
    d. Love, hope, and faithfulness

12. The carol "Noël nouvelet!" refers to Mary making an offering on behalf of the Baby Jesus forty days after his birth. What was the offering?
    a. A lamb
    b. A chicken
    c. A fish
    d. A pair of turtledoves

13. The French version of "Winter Wonderland" is called "Au royaume du bonhomme hiver." What does the French title mean?
    a. In the kingdom of the winter snowman
    b. The happy world of winter
    c. The royal winter palace
    d. Good men, come join our winter festival

14. What Oscar-winning actor narrated an audiobook about the writing of "Silent Night"?
    a. Paul Newman
    b. Sir Laurence Olivier
    c. Mickey Rooney
    d. Robert Duvall

15. "Silent Night" was first performed in 1818, but in what year was it written, according to a manuscript reproduced on the website of the Silent Night Museum?

   a. 1770   b. 1816   c. 1896   d. 1922

Plum Puddings

16. According to the French government website, France Diplomatie, in what century were Christmas carols first sung in that country?

   a. Fourteenth   c. Sixteenth
   b. Fifteenth   d. Seventeenth

17. The composer of the music for "O Holy Night" also wrote many operas and ballets, including *Faust* and *Giselle*. Who was he?

   a. Adolphe Adam   c. Jacques Offenbach
   b. Claude Debussy   d. Leo Delibes

18. The sixteenth century carol "Bring a Torch, Jeanette, Isabella" originated in which region of France?

   a. Provence   b. Lorraine   c. Normandy   d. Alsace

19. What is the name of the French-language version of "The First Nowell"?

    a. "La premiere Noël"
    b. "Aujourd'hui le roi des cieux"
    c. "Ah! Quel grand mystère!"
    d. "Noël nouvelet!"

20. Which famous French painter depicted a nativity scene based on the carol, "Bring a Torch, Jeanette, Isabella"?

    a. Pierre-Auguste Renoir   c. Georges LaTour
    b. Claude Monet   d. Edgar Degas

21. Which two nativity scene animals are the subjects of "The Burgundian Carol"?

    a. Sheep and cow   c. Camel and rooster
    b. Ox and donkey   d. Dove and nightingale

22. What lively carol that originated in France has a chorus that uses a similar melismatic sequence for the word "Gloria" as that in "Angels We Have Heard on High"?

    a. "I Saw Three Ships"
    b. "Ding Dong! Merrily on High"
    c. "Christians, Awake!"
    d. "Joy to the World"

23. The melody to "O Tannenbaum" is the state song for three U.S. states. Which of these is not one of them?

    a. Ohio   b. Michigan   c. Iowa   d. Maryland

24. The Silent Night Museum is located in the birthplace of Joseph Mohr, the priest who wrote the words to the carol. In what city is it located?

    a. Vienna   b. Innsbruck   c. Salzburg   d. Linz

25. What beloved carol was banned for more than two decades from being sung in Catholic churches in France, apparently because the composer was thought to be Jewish?

    a. "O Holy Night"
    b. "Angels We Have Heard on High"
    c. "Ave Maria"
    d. "Quittez pasteurs"

26. The author of the poem "Minuit, chrétiens," which became the lyrics for "O Holy Night," was an amateur writer. How did he make his living?

    a. Eel fishing   c. Wine selling
    b. Gold mining   d. Carpet cleaning

27. "I Saw Three Ships" is a popular carol in English-speaking countries. What is the most commonly sung German carol that tells of Jesus arriving on a ship?

a. "A Ship in the Morning"
b. "The Saviour's Ship"
c. "A Ship Rode on the Christmas Tide"
d. "There Comes a Ship a-Sailing"

28. What German carol was described by George Bernard Shaw as sounding like "the funeral march of a dead eel"?

a. "O Tannenbaum"
b. "Silent Night"
c. "Come, All Ye Shepherds"
d. "Joseph Dearest, Joseph Mine"

29. The music for what French carol is based on a Norman hunting tune?

a. "Entre le boeuf et l'âne gris"   c. "Il est né, le divin enfant!"
b. "Quittez pasteurs"   d. "Dans cette etable"

30. A traditional French carol refers to the Baby Jesus as being watched over by what or whom?

a. Joseph and Mary   c. Oxen and asses
b. Angels   d. Stars

31. Which political movement is referenced in the English translation of the French carol, "O Holy Night" ("Cantique de Noël")?

    a. Anarchism
    b. Women's suffrage
    c. Abolitionism
    d. Anti-colonialism

32. Which famous German wrote the Christmas carol "Vom Himmel hoch da komm ich her" ("From Heaven Above I Come to You")?

    a. Martin Luther
    b. Marlene Dietrich
    c. Johann Sebastian Bach
    d. Karl Marx

33. For what occasion was "Vom Himmel hoch da komm ich her" ("From Heaven Above I Come to You") written?

    a. Midnight mass
    b. Advent
    c. A family Christmas celebration
    d. The birth of a son

Chestnuts

34. What Provençal carol is sung to a tune that was originally written as a military victory march?

    a. "Bring a Torch, Jeanette, Isabella"
    b. "Far Away, What Splendour Comes This Way?"
    c. "O Holy Night"
    d. "Angels We Have Heard on High"

35. Carols have sometimes been inspired by unlikely events. Two were written by Philipp Nicolai, a German pastor, in the wake of a bubonic plague that ravaged his town and moved him to contemplate the afterlife. Name one of them. (Double points if you get both.)

   a. "Wie Schön Leuchtet des Morgenstern"
      ("How Fair the Morning Star Doth Shine")
   b. "Wachet Auf!" ("Wake, O Wake")
   c. "Christum Wir Sollen Loben Schön"
      ("From Lands That See the Sun Arise")
   d. "Es Steht ein Lind im Himmelreich"
      ("There Stood in Heaven a Linden Tree")

36. In what year was the first recording of "Silent Night" made?
   a. 1895   b. 1905   c. 1915   d. 1925

37. Which French carol dating back perhaps as far as the sixteenth century is believed by some scholars to have been the inspiration for "The Little Drummer Boy"?

   a. "Noël nouvelet!"   c. "Pat-a-pan"
   b. "Dans cette etable"   d. "Quittez pasteurs"

38. Many carols were originally written as poems, which were later set to music. This carol reversed the process. The tune was originally written as a dance composition by a sixteenth century French priest named Jehan Tabourot. It was not provided with lyrics until the twentieth century and has since become one of the most popular carols at Christmas. What is it?

   a. "Ding Dong! Merrily on High"
   b. "Carol of the Bells"
   c. "Caroling, Caroling"
   d. "Do You Hear What I Hear?"

39. What European carol was sung on Christmas episodes of *South Park* and *Studio 60 on the Sunset Strip*?

   a. "O Tannenbaum"   c. "O Come All Ye Faithful"
   b. "O Holy Night"   d. "O Leave Your Sheep"

40. What carol was written by a German pastor who was named poet laureate in 1645 by Emperor Ferdinand III?

   a. "From Heaven High"
   b. "From Lands That See the Sun Arise"
   c. "Break Forth, O Beauteous Heavenly Light"
   d. "O Sleep, Thou Heaven-Born Treasure, Thou"

41. What Franco-Germanic carol was voted the favourite by British listeners to a classic FM radio station in 2006?

    a. "Silent Night"   c. "Ave Maria"
    b. "Away in a Manger"   d. "O Holy Night"

42. What traditional French carol was incorporated into his *L'Arlésienne Suites* by the great composer Georges Bizet?

    a. "Far Away, What Splendour Comes This Way?"
    b. "Bring a Torch, Jeanette, Isabella"
    c. "Noël nouvelet!"
    d. "Angels We Have Heard on High"

43. What musical instrument was used to play "O Holy Night," the first carol ever broadcast on radio, in 1906?

    a. Piano   b. Flute   c. Harp   d. Violin

44. Whose death is said to have been part of the inspiration for Joseph Mohr to write "Silent Night"?

    a. His mother's   c. His father's
    b. His sister's   d. His grandfather's

45. What early French carol was recorded by The Weavers?

  a. "The Burgundian Carol"
  b. "O Holy Night"
  c. "Bring a Torch Jeanette, Isabella"
  d. "Ding Dong! Merrily on High"

46. The carol "Angels We Have Heard on High" is believed to have originated in what part of France?

  a. Burgundy   b. Savoy   c. Normandy   d. Lorraine

47. "Noël nouvelet!" is a traditional French carol known in English by several different names. Which of the following is *not* one of these names?

  a. "Christmas Comes Anew"   c. "Sing We Now of Christmas"
  b. "Noël! A New Noël!"   d. "Yule Tidings"

48. The traditional French carol "Whence Is That Goodly Fragrance?" ("Quelle est cette odeur agreable?") was likely inspired by which nativity legend?

  a. Legend of the talking animals
  b. Legend of the Christmas star
  c. Legend of the cobwebs
  d. Legend of the Christmas bloom

49. Which famed nineteenth century German composer arranged a series of carols into a piano solo entitled "Christmas Tree Suite"?

    a. Mendelssohn   c. Beethoven

    b. Liszt   d. Bach

50. Name the sixteenth century traditional French carol whose title imitates the sound of a drum being played.

    a. "Pat-a-pan"   c. "Tap-a-tap"

    b. "Boom-ba-boom"   d. "Zing-a-zang"

51. "Noël des enfants qui n'ont plus de maisons" ("Christmas Carol for Homeless Children") is an angry song that asks the Baby Jesus to punish France's enemies and avenge the children of war. It was composed during the dark days of the First World War by which famous composer?

    a. Georges Bizet   c. Erik Satie

    b. Claude Debussy   d. Camille Saint-Saëns

52. "Berger secoue ton sommeil profond" is a traditional French carol. The title calls upon which nativity character to "awake from your drowsy sleep"?

    a. Innkeeper   b. Wise man   c. Shepherd   d. Angel

53. "While By My Sheep" ("Als Ich Bei Meinen Schafen Wacht")
is a traditional German carol dating back to the Middle Ages.
Because of the repeated refrains, it is sometimes known as
what?

a. "The Ditto Carol"   c. "The Memory Carol"
b. "The Echo Carol"   d. "The Two-Two Carol"

54. The music for which carol was in part based on a German
melody written by Felix Mendelssohn to honour the four
hundredth anniversary of the Gutenberg printing press?

a. "O Tannenbaum"
b. "O Come All Ye Faithful"
c. "Hark! The Herald Angels Sing"
d. "Away in a Manger"

Did You Know?

Plague, Death, and Two Carols

The years 1597 and 1598 were terrible times in the German province of Westphalia. Bubonic plague—the "Black Death"—swept through the region taking hundreds of lives and leaving whole towns devastated. In the town of Unna, the local pastor, Philipp Nicolai, comforted the dying and presided over or witnessed more than two dozen burials a day at the height of the outbreak. It is said that he lost more than thirteen hundred of his parishioners.

One of the last victims of the scourge was the fifteen-year-old Count of Waldech, whom Nicolai had tutored from the time he was five and whom he dearly loved. The pastor deeply grieved the loss of his young pupil but at the same time was inspired by his death to write two joyous carols that celebrate the afterlife and are popular in Germany to this day.

In "Wachet Auf!", translated as "Wake, O Wake," we read the line: "Now rise we all to that glad hall, where to thy feast thou dost us call," which refers to the count and the other victims ascending to heaven. In "Wie Schön Leuchtet der Morgenstern" ("How Fair the Morning Star Doth Shine"), Nicolai describes what may be the meeting of the young count with Christ with these words:

A heavenly light upon me plays
When Christ on me doth turn his gaze,
With loving eyes to view me;
Thy precious Word and Spirit, Lord,
Thy body broken, blood outpoured,
Sustain me and renew me.
Hold me, fold me
Gently to thee;
Warm me thoroughly;
O espouse me
With what gifts thy Word endows me!

The "Silent Night" Story

It's difficult to distinguish myth from fact when searching for the origins of the classic carol "Silent Night." The widely accepted story is that the curate of St. Nicholas church in the Austrian mountain village of Oberndorf was appalled to discover that the organ wouldn't play as he was making last-minute preparations for midnight mass on Christmas Eve, 1818. According to some versions, the organ had rusted, although it's difficult to imagine how that might have happened since the church was in regular use. Others say it had simply died of old age, while still other accounts suggest that mice or squirrels had been gnawing away at its bellows. Whatever the case, the curate,

Joseph Mohr, had the equivalent of a panic attack. The flock would be arriving in a few hours and there would be no music!

In desperation, he grabbed a Christmas poem that he had written a couple of years earlier from his desk and rushed to the home of the church's assistant organist, Franz Gruber. He implored Gruber to set his simple words to music in a form that could be quickly learned by the choir and played on a guitar. Some chroniclers credit divine intervention for Gruber's ability to compose the classic melody in the space of only a few hours. Whatever his inspiration, what was destined to become one of the world's favourite carols was performed for the first time that night in the small church and the mass was saved.

. However, one of the most scholarly works on the history of carols suggests this lovely story is "more fable than fact." Hugh Keyte and Andrew Parrott, authors of *The New Oxford Book of Carols,* say that in their research they could find no contemporary accounts that confirmed there was any problem with the church organ and that in reality it remained in use for many years afterward.

The story doesn't end there. For many years, the true origin of "Silent Night" was shrouded in mystery. Because Joseph Mohr did not sign his name to the original music, it became accepted throughout the region that the carol was a Tyrolean folk song. According to one story, it was only when the king of Prussia, who had been deeply moved by the beauty of the song, sent a team of investigators to the region that the true authorship was revealed.

However it came about, it was several decades before Mohr and Gruber were officially recognized as the real writers of the lovely hymn that has become a standard in Christmas celebrations around the world.

Wine, Ballet, Abolitionism, and Radio— The Story of "O Holy Night"

The story behind "O Holy Night" is filled with so many strange twists and turns that it's sometimes difficult to separate fact from myth. If we are to believe all the tales that have come down to us over the past century and a half, this lovely French carol was the unlikely creation of a wine merchant and a great composer, was banned by the Roman Catholic Church, became a theme for abolitionists in North America, temporarily stopped a war, and was the first piece of music ever broadcast by radio. That's quite a resumé!

According to most accounts, the carol's genesis began in 1847 in the French town of Roquemaure, not far from Avignon. The town's mayor, Placide Clappeau (sometimes also spelled Cappeau), who was by trade a wine merchant and by avocation an occasional poet, was asked by the parish priest to write a poem to be read at Christmas midnight mass. Clappeau, who never wrote anything memorable before or after, used the Gospel of Luke as his inspiration to write a work he called "Minuit, chrétiens" ("Midnight, Christians").

Some versions of the story say that the poem was written while Clappeau was travelling to Paris by stagecoach or train (take your pick). There the wine merchant met with the famous composer Adolph Adam, who had written numerous operas and ballets, including *Giselle*. Here again, accounts disagree on how exactly this meeting came about or why a man of Adam's stature would be interested in the writings of an amateur from a small town in Provence (according to some versions, the two were introduced by a mutual acquaintance). But there is no doubting the fact that Adam (who, ironically, was of Jewish heritage) was so taken with the lyrics that he undertook to compose the music to what has become one of the world's best-loved carols.

"O Holy Night" was what we would today describe as an instant hit among the French. But then the leaders of the Roman Catholic Church decided that the song, in the words of one bishop, displayed a "total absence of the spirit of religion" (this despite the fact that the lyrics were obviously based on Luke's gospel) and banned it from services. The real reason, many suspect, was Adam's Jewish background, although when he died he was buried as a Christian.

So, in effect, "O Holy Night" was driven underground in the country of its origin. Across the Atlantic, however, something very different was happening. In 1855, a New England clergyman, John Sullivan Dwight, is reputed to have translated the carol into English, although the precise date has been called into question. His version of the lyrics contained the following lines, which are an approximate translation from Clappeau's original:

Chains shall He break for the slave is our brother;
And in His name all oppression shall cease.

Dwight was a strong advocate of abolition, an issue that was dividing the United States at the time and which eventually led to the Civil War. "O Holy Night" became a favourite hymn among abolitionists and was widely sung in the North (but rarely, if ever, in the southern states) during this difficult period.

The carol is said to have played a role in another war a few years later—the Franco–Prussian War of 1870–71. Although no definitive proof has ever been produced, legend has it that on Christmas Eve, 1870, an unknown French soldier emerged from his trench and stood in the no man's land between the opposing forces singing the carol. The German side was so moved that they sent one of their own into the battlefield to sing Martin Luther's "Vom Himmel hoch da komm ich her" ("From Heaven Above I Come to You"). Who knows if it actually happened, but it makes for a terrific story.

Now flash forward a generation. It is Christmas Eve, 1906, and a Canadian-born inventor, Reginald Fessenden, is about to make history. Fessenden worked with Thomas Edison for a time and eventually became interested in the new science of radio. Working for the U.S. Weather Bureau, he is believed to have been the first person to transmit a voice signal by radio waves in December 1900. He continued his work in the field in collaboration with General Electric, and on Christmas Eve, 1906, he made the first entertainment radio broadcast from his facility in Brant Rock, Massachusetts. The evening's highlight: Fessenden's violin rendition of "O Holy Night."

So the next time you hear a rendition of this stirring carol, pause for a moment to contemplate the inspiring words and to remember the remarkable history of this beautiful hymn.

American Carols

The writing of Christmas carols in the United States reached its zenith in the mid-nineteenth century, around the time of the Civil War. In fact, many of the carols that are popular to this day were inspired in some way by that terrible conflict or by the events that immediately preceded it.

In retrospect, the nineteenth century was the only period during which American writers and composers created memorable religious-based carols. "It Came Upon a Midnight Clear," "O Little Town of Bethlehem," "Away in a Manger," "I Heard the Bells on Christmas Day," and "We Three Kings of Orient Are" all date from this period, as do such popular secular holiday songs as "Jingle Bells."

Prior to that time, Puritanism stifled joyful Christmas music and only a few carols were written, mainly in the latter part of the eighteenth century. During the twentieth century, the emphasis shifted almost entirely to secular Christmas tunes, which composers turned out by the dozens—everything from "White Christmas" to "All I Want for Christmas Is My Two Front Teeth." But not a single classic American hymn-type carol was written in that century.

So, amazing as it may seem, virtually all of America's great carols were written within a span of less than twenty-five years, from 1849 to 1872. After that, carol writing in the United States seemed to become a lost art until Alfred Burt revived it in the 1940s.

Brainteaser Trivia

(Answers on page 217)

Pumpkin Pies

1. How are the plains described in the second verse of "It Came Upon a Midnight Clear"?

   a. Flat and desolate   c. Broad and boundless

   b. Sad and lowly   d. Rich and fertile

2. What spiritual carol contains the lyrics: "We didn't know who You was"?

   a. "Sweet Little Jesus Boy"   c. "Go Tell It on the Mountain"

   b. "Mary Had a Baby"   d. "I Wonder as I Wander"

3. Many carols were originally written as poems and later set to music. Which of the following American carols was *not* composed first as a poem?

   a. "It Came Upon a Midnight Clear"

   b. "O Little Town of Bethlehem"

   c. "I Heard the Bells on Christmas Day"

   d. "We Three Kings of Orient Are"

4. To which great religious leader were the lyrics of "Away in a Manger" mistakenly attributed?
   a. John Calvin
   b. Martin Luther
   c. The apostle Paul
   d. John Knox

5. What was the first carol to be broadcast from space?
   a. "Silent Night"
   b. "Jingle Bells"
   c. "Away in a Manger"
   d. "O Little Town of Bethlehem"

6. How are the skies described in the second verse of "It Came Upon a Midnight Clear"?
   a. Dark'ning   b. Cloven   c. Golden   d. Bright'ning

7. Which carol makes reference to a train in the last line in describing the nativity?
   a. "Rise Up, Shepherd, and Follow"
   b. "It Came Upon a Midnight Clear"
   c. "Mary Had a Baby"
   d. "I Wonder as I Wander"

8. What great American poet wrote the words to "I Heard the Bells on Christmas Day"?
   a. Henry Wadsworth Longfellow
   b. Walt Whitman
   c. Edgar Allan Poe
   d. Robert Frost

9. In "We Three Kings of Orient Are," what does myrrh symbolize?

a. Life   b. Death   c. Wealth   d. God

10. In the second verse of "O Little Town of Bethlehem," what is said to "proclaim the holy birth"?

a. Angels   c. Morning stars

b. Heavens above   d. Meek souls

11. Many of the great Negro spirituals were inspired by the hardships of slavery, but only a few specifically relate to Christmas. Of these, "Go Tell It on the Mountain" is the best known. Which of the following spirituals also relates to Christmas?

a. "Rise Up, Shepherd, and Follow"

b. "Swing Low, Sweet Chariot"

c. "There Is a Balm in Gilead"

d. "My Good Lord Done Been Here"

12. What holiday was "Jingle Bells" originally written to celebrate?

a. Christmas   c. New Year's

b. Thanksgiving   d. Independence Day

13. The inspiration for "We Three Kings of Orient Are" came from which gospel?

a. Matthew   b. Mark   c. Luke   d. John

14. Based on the modern calendar, the Three Kings of the carol arrived on January 6. What is the religious name of that day?

    a. Advent   b. Ascension   c. Epiphany   d. Assumption

15. What attribute that is ascribed to the Baby Jesus in "Away in a Manger" would be welcomed by most modern parents?

    a. He sleeps on hay   c. He is watched over by animals
    b. He doesn't cry   d. He wakes easily

16. The chorus of "We Three Kings of Orient Are" contains a line that begins: "Star of wonder …." There are several versions of what follows. Which one is recognized as correct by *The New Oxford Book of Carols*?

    a. Star so bright   c. Star of right
    b. Star of night   d. Star of light

17. American composer George Frederick Root, who wrote a long-forgotten carol, was named after a great European composer whose music has become part of our Christmas tradition. Who was he?

    a. Debussy   b. Bach   c. Handel   d. Mozart

18. In what year did two astronauts use a harmonica and sleigh bells to deliver a space rendition of "Jingle Bells"?

    a. 1993   b. 1986   c. 1971   d. 1965

Plum Puddings

19. In an often-overlooked verse from "Jingle Bells," what misfortune befalls the singer?

   a. He gets kicked by the horse
   b. He falls on his back in the snow
   c. Miss Fanny Bright gets angry with him
   d. He gets lost

20. What carol was written by a newspaper reporter who was also a clergyman?

   a. "O Little Town of Bethlehem"
   b. "It Came Upon a Midnight Clear"
   c. "We Three Kings of Orient Are"
   d. "Jingle Bells"

21. What American carol has been sung to several tunes, one of which is the Scottish melody "Flow Gently Sweet Afton"?

   a. "Away in a Manger"
   b. "I Heard the Bells on Christmas Day"
   c. "O Little Town of Bethlehem"
   d. "It Came Upon a Midnight Clear"

22. What was the name of the poem by Longfellow that eventually became the lyrics for "I Heard the Bells on Christmas Day"?

   a. "The Bells"
   b. "Christmas Bells"
   c. "Hark, The Bells"
   d. "The Bells Proclaim the Saviour's Birth"

23. What was Abraham Lincoln's favourite carol?

   a. "Away in a Manger"
   b. "We Three Kings of Orient Are"
   c. "Christians, Awake!"
   d. "What Child Is This?"

24. What carol inspired an annual run in support of arthritis research?

   a. "The Twelve Days of Christmas"
   b. "Jingle Bells"
   c. "Go Tell It on the Mountain"
   d. "Have Yourself a Merry Little Christmas"

25. The writer of which American carol had a building named in his honour at Harvard University?

   a. "We Three Kings of Orient Are"
   b. "Glory to God on High"
   c. "O Little Town of Bethlehem"
   d. "As Shepherds in Jewry"

26. In the lyrics of "Jingle Bells," what is the speed of the horse?

   a. Two-forty
   b. Three-fifty
   c. Forty-two
   d. High-stepping five

27. What carol has lyrics that speak directly to the horrors of the Civil War, including references to cannons, hate, and the South?

   a. "Ye Nations All, On You I Call"
   b. "I Heard the Bells on Christmas Day"
   c. "Christmas on the Sea"
   d. "It Came Upon a Midnight Clear"

28. Which carol had its lyrics written by a minister who doubled as an editor, and its music composed by a New York newspaper critic?

   a. "Angels from the Realms of Glory"
   b. "Glory to God on High"
   c. "It Came Upon a Midnight Clear"
   d. "As Shepherds in Jewry"

29. What was the original title of "Jingle Bells"?

   a. "Dashing Through the Snow"
   b. "Sleigh Ride"
   c. "One Horse Open Sleigh"
   d. "Bells on Bob-Tail"

30. Where in the world are people who travel in a sleigh on a highway required by law to have at least two bells attached to the harness?

    a. Massachusetts   c. Scotland
    b. Ontario, Canada   d. Alaska

31. What carol's composer was the uncle of famed Wall Street financier J.P. Morgan?

    a. "Jingle Bells"
    b. "O Little Town of Bethlehem"
    c. "Go Tell It on the Mountain"
    d. "Ye Nations All, On You I Call"

32. The words to "It Came Upon a Midnight Clear" were first published in which magazine?

    a. *Atlantic Monthly*   c. *Century Magazine*
    b. *Church Weekly*   d. *Christian Register*

33. The day of the funeral of the author of one of America's greatest carols was proclaimed as a day of mourning in Massachusetts. Who was the writer?

    a. Phillips Brooks   c. Supply Belcher
    b. William Billings   d. Edmund Sears

34. Which carol, sometimes attributed to Appalachian folk music, actually dates back to medieval England?

    a. "Mary Had a Baby"
    b. "As Joseph Was A-Walking"
    c. "Rise Up, Shepherd, and Follow"
    d. "Go Tell It on the Mountain"

35. A melody written by American composer William Billings was used in the carol "Shepherds, Rejoice!" to set the words of English hymnist Isaac Watts to music. What was the original name of the Billings composition?

    a. "Night"   b. "Rivers"   c. "Boston"   d. "The Sea"

36. Which carol, whose lyrics were written at the height of the Civil War, contains this line: "And in despair, I bowed my head: There is no peace on earth, I said"?

    a. "It Came Upon a Midnight Clear"
    b. "I Heard the Bells on Christmas Day"
    c. "O Little Town of Bethlehem"
    d. "We Three Kings of Orient Are"

Chestnuts

37. Biographers have called the composer of "As Shepherds in Jewry" "a gargoyle" because he had only one eye, a withered arm, and a shortened leg. What was his name?
    a. Supply Belcher
    b. William Billings
    c. William Walker
    d. William Gifford

38. Which of these carols was written by Phillips Brooks, author of the lyrics to "O Little Town of Bethlehem"?
    a. "Glad Christmas Tidings"
    b. "Christmas by the Fire"
    c. "Everywhere, Everywhere, Christmas Tonight"
    d. "Snow Through the Canopy of Light"

39. The rector of New York's Trinity Church wrote one of the earliest American carols, entitled "Shout the Glad Tidings." Later, he wrote martial hymns to inspire soldiers in the Union army during the Civil War. Who was he?
    a. James Ramsey Murray
    b. Edmund Hamilton Sears
    c. Henry Wadsworth Longfellow
    d. William Augustus Muhlenberg

40. The author of "O Little Town of Bethlehem" delivered an oration at the lying in state of which American president?
    a. William McKinley
    b. Abraham Lincoln
    c. Thomas Jefferson
    d. Franklin D. Roosevelt

41. The composer of "The Lord Descended from Above" earned the nickname "The Handel of Maine" because of his musical style. Who was he?

a. Phillips Brooks

b. William Billings

c. Supply Belcher

d. Jeremiah Ingalls

42. William Walker, who wrote the carol "Ye Nations All, On You I Call," lived most of his life in the small town of Spartanburg, South Carolina. Two other residents of the town were also named William Walker and went by the nicknames "Hog Billy" and "Pig Billy." What name was used to identify the composer?

a. "Fiddle Billy"

b. "Singing Billy"

c. "Music Billy"

d. "Happy Billy"

43. Which early American composer was operating a tavern in Newbury, Vermont, when he wrote the carol "Glory to God on High"?

a. William Billings

b. John Henry Hopkins Jr.

c. Jeremiah Ingalls

d. Edmund Sears

44. What American carol that is seldom heard today is said to have been the favourite of American president Andrew Jackson?
    a. "The Lord Descended from Above"
    b. "Shout the Glad Tidings"
    c. "The Sky Can Still Remember"
    d. "Gather Round the Christmas Tree"

45. Henry Hopkins Jr. wrote "We Three Kings of Orient Are" as a Christmas gift for whom?
    a. His children
    b. His grandchildren
    c. His nephews and nieces
    d. Local orphans

46. The writer of one of America's most beloved carols once said: "Christianity helps us face the music even when we don't like the tune." Who was he?
    a. Phillips Brooks
    b. William Walker
    c. William Billings
    d. Henry Hopkins Jr.

47. In Britain, "O Little Town of Bethlehem" is sung to a different tune than in North America, one based on an English folk melody. What is the name of that melody?
    a. "The River Bank"
    b. "The Ploughboy's Dream"
    c. "Starry Night"
    d. "The Moor"

48. Phillips Brooks, the writer of "O Little Town of Bethlehem," also penned another carol, which has been virtually forgotten over time. What was its name?

    a. "The Lowly Stable"
    b. "Mary Watched the Newborn Babe"
    c. "Come Greet the Glorious Day"
    d. "The Sky Can Still Remember"

49. The writer of which carol has remained a mystery to scholars and probably will never be known with certainty?

    a. "Away in a Manger"
    b. "We Three Kings of Orient Are"
    c. "It Came Upon a Midnight Clear"
    d. "As Shepherds in Jewry"

50. Which carol was written by an American poet and set to music by an English composer?

    a. "God Rest Ye Merry, Gentlemen"
    b. "The First Nowell"
    c. "Joy to the World"
    d. "I Heard the Bells on Christmas Day"

51. What carol of unknown origin was preserved only because a singer who was also a collector of folk songs paid a little girl twenty-five cents to sing it for him at the height of the Depression?

    a. "I Wonder as I Wander"   c. "Mary Had a Baby"

    b. "Mary, Did You Know?"   d. "Sing We the Virgin Mary"

52. Henry Hopkins Jr., who wrote "We Three Kings of Orient Are," later composed another carol that has long since been forgotten. What was its name?

    a. "Christ the King"

    b. "Gather Round the Christmas Tree"

    c. "The Blessed Stable"

    d. "The Miracle of Christmas"

53. The lyrics to these carols were all written around the middle of the nineteenth century. What was the last one to be set to music?

    a. "I Heard the Bells on Christmas Day"

    b. "O Little Town of Bethlehem"

    c. "It Came Upon a Midnight Clear"

    d. "Jingle Bells"

54. George Fredrick Root is best remembered for his stirring Civil War songs—such as "Tramp, Tramp, Tramp," "Just Before the Battle, Mother," and "The Battle Cry of Freedom." But he also co-wrote a carol that was included in the Burl Ives album "Christmas at the White House" as the favourite of Theodore Roosevelt. What was its name?

a. "Christmas on the Battle Field"
b. "Christmas Far From Home"
c. "My Boy's Last Christmas"
d. "Christmas at Sea"

55. What obscure American carol was praised by Oliver Wendell Holmes as one of "the most beautiful ever written"?

a. "Gather Round the Christmas Tree"
b. "Christmas at Sea"
c. "Calm on the List'ning Ear of Night"
d. "As Shepherds in Jewry"

Did You Know?

The Musical Gargoyle

William Billings was about as unlikely a composer as you'll find in history. He was born in 1746 into a poor New England family. He had no education to speak of and earned his living mainly as a tanner for many years, although he also at times held such unusual positions as "hog reeve." He was physically disabled—some biographers have referred to him as "a gargoyle"—with one blind eye, a withered arm, and a shortened leg. He seems to have had little regard for personal hygiene and is said to have consumed copious amounts of snuff. He learned music on his own, with no formal training. Yet this strange man was a friend to such giants of the American Revolution as Sam Adams and Paul Revere, was a pioneer of early American music, and was the composer of numerous hymns and anthems, including the carol "As Shepherds in Jewry."

An article published in *Atlantic Monthly* in 1882 described his influence this way: "Billings invented a new way of setting hymns and anthems, which was called the fuguing style. It became extremely popular because of its vivacity, the voice parts moving in a sort of mutual imitation (not fugue properly), in quick time, chasing one another round.... Here was a music that was found exciting; a lively rhythmical protest (for men had been drinking of the new wine of liberty) against the dry and dreary old music; a music flattering to the sense and a relief to the imprisoned spirit."

One of Billings's compositions, entitled "Chester," became the unofficial anthem of the thirteen American colonies during the Revolutionary War. Although it has long since been forgotten, the lyrics are stirring. Some sample verses:

Let tyrants shake their iron rods,
And Slav'ry clank her galling chains.
We fear them not, we trust in God.
New England's God forever reigns.
Howe and Burgoyne and Clinton, too,
With Prescott and Cornwallis joined,
Together plot our overthrow,
In one infernal league combined.
When God inspired us for the fight,
Their ranks were broke, their lines were forced,
Their ships were shattered in our sight,
Or swiftly driven from our coast.
The foe comes on with haughty stride,
Our troops advance with martial noise;
Their vet'rans flee before our youth,
And gen'rals yield to beardless boys.

Soldiers and Tavernkeepers

Although many early American carol composers were men of the church, a surprising number came from backgrounds that seem incongruous with the writing of religious music. During our research, we were startled to discover how many carols had been written by veterans of the Revolutionary War and supporters of the North in the Civil War. We were also surprised to find that many carol composers had at one time or another been associated with the manufacture or sale of alcohol.

One man who qualified on both counts carried the unfortunate name of Supply Belcher. He was born in Massachusetts in 1751 or 1752 (sources differ) and was among the minutemen at the Battle of Lexington. He eventually became a captain in George Washington's army.

After the war, he became a tavernkeeper in Canton where, according to Wikipedia, he became known as "Uncle Ply." The tavern must have been a jolly spot since history tells us it became a meeting place for musicians.

Although both he and William Billings ("The Musical Gargoyle") were contemporaries in the same area of Massachusetts, there is no evidence that Belcher ever studied with him.

Belcher subsequently moved with his family to Maine and it was there that he became seriously involved with music, although he never worked as a musician full-time. His works were so elaborate and harmonious that he became known as "The Handel of Maine." A local reverend, Paul Coffin, wrote at the time: "Squire Belcher called his singers together and gave us an evening of sweet music."

The carol for which he was best known is entitled "The Lord Descended from Above." The words are based on Psalm 18, verses nine and ten:

> The Lord descended from above,
> And bow'd the heavens most high,
> And underneath his feet he cast
> The darkness of the sky.
> On cherubs and on cherubims
> Full royally he rode,
> And on the wings of mighty winds
> Came flying, flying, flying all abroad.

The carol was very popular in Puritan New England but is rarely heard today, and Belcher's name has been all but forgotten except by music scholars.

A Dead President and a Timeless Carol

Phillips Brooks became known as the greatest American preacher of the nineteenth century before he died in 1893. His career as a clergyman included a long period as the rector of historic Trinity Church in

Boston and later as the Episcopalian Bishop of Massachusetts. So great was his influence at the time that an article published in *Atlantic Monthly* shortly after his death placed him on the same pedestal as such literary giants as Goethe, Tennyson, and Longfellow, going so far as to say that "he was in some respects the greatest of them all."

In fact, few people today would recognize the name of Phillips Brooks, but we unknowingly remember him every Christmas. His legacy to the modern world came as a result of the events that occurred during the seven years from 1862 to 1869 while he was rector at the Church of the Holy Trinity in Philadelphia. It was during that time that Brooks penned what was to become one of America's most beloved carols: "O Little Town of Bethlehem." The tragic irony in the story is that the carol might never have been written had it not been for the assassination of one of the greatest presidents in U.S. history, Abraham Lincoln.

Brooks was a staunch opponent of slavery and frequently denounced the practice in his sermons. While an outspoken supporter of the Northern cause, he was deeply distressed by the slaughter of the Civil War, which was raging at the time. He saw the embattled Lincoln as the embodiment of all that was good about America and was devastated when the president was murdered by John Wilkes Booth at Ford's Theater on the night of April 14, 1865—ironically, Good Friday, the day that Jesus was crucified. As the body of the slain president was lying in state in Philadelphia, Brooks delivered an impassioned (and very long) oration over the casket in which he described Lincoln as a force for good in a world of evil. His stirring words were preserved for posterity in the posthumous publication of six of his greatest sermons and speeches in 1895.

"If ever anything were clear, this is the clearest," Brooks proclaimed during the solemn ceremony.

Is there the man alive who thinks that Abraham Lincoln was shot just for himself; that it was that one man for whom the plot was laid? The gentlest, kindest, most indulgent man that ever ruled a State! The man who knew not how to speak a word of harshness or how to make a foe! Was it he for whom the murderer lurked with a mere private hate? It was not he, but what he stood for. It was Law and Liberty, it was Government and Freedom, against which the hate gathered and the treacherous shot was fired. And I know not how the crime of him who shoots at Law and Liberty in the crowded glare of a great theater differs from theirs who have leveled their aim at the same great beings from behind a thousand ambuscades and on a hundred battle-fields of this long war. Every general in the field, and every false citizen in our midst at home, who has plotted and labored to destroy the lives of the soldiers of the Republic, is brother to him who did this deed. The American nature, the American truths, of which our President was the anointed and supreme embodiment, have been embodied in multitudes of heroes who marched unknown and fell unnoticed in our ranks. For them, just as for him, character decreed a life and a death. The blood of all of them I charge on the same head. Slavery armed with Treason was their murderer ....

Referring to Lincoln's Gettysburg Address, he concluded the tribute by saying:

He stood once on the battle-field of our own State, and said of the brave men who had saved it words as noble as any countryman of ours ever spoke. Let us stand in the country he has saved, and which is to be his grave and monument, and say of Abraham Lincoln what he said of the soldiers who had died at Gettysburg ... "The world will little note nor long remember what we say here, but it can never forget what they did here."

After the funeral, Brooks was left emotionally drained and dispirited—today we would describe him as "burnt out." Feeling the need to escape from the ravaged nation, he took a sabbatical and travelled to Europe and later to the Middle East, seeking spiritual rebirth by walking in Christ's footsteps. He found his new beginning on a hill outside of Bethlehem. In the journal he kept during his travels, he described how he rode on horseback from Jerusalem to the remote village and stood on Christmas Eve in the same field where the angel is believed to have appeared to the shepherds.

The peace and beauty of the scene remained with him when he returned to Philadelphia, reinvigorated, to resume his preaching. Three years after his pilgrimage to Bethlehem, he put the images in his mind to paper in the form of a poem during the Christmas season of 1868 (some scholars dispute this time frame, claiming he jotted down the poem on the same night he stood in the field near Bethlehem). His church organist set the words to music—the story is that the inspiration for the melody came to him in a dream on Christmas Eve—and so was born the lovely, reverent carol we now sing every year at Christmastime.

The Mysterious Child

Among all the strange and unusual stories about Christmas carols, perhaps none is stranger than the tale of how "I Wonder as I Wander" came to be part of our yuletide celebrations.

The year was 1933, at the height of the Great Depression. John Jacob Niles, a singer and a collector of American folk music, found himself in the town of Murphy, North Carolina, on a warm July day. In notes written later, he tells of how he came across the family of a revivalist preacher named Morgan who had set up camp in the town square, much to the displeasure of the local officials. The Morgans had been ordered to leave by the police but pleaded poverty and asked to stage one more revival meeting to raise enough money to pay for gas for their dilapidated vehicle.

It was at that point that Niles happened upon the scene, just as one of the preacher's children, a girl named Annie, appeared. Niles described her as "a tousled, unwashed blond, and very lovely."

She began to sing a song he had never before heard: "I Wonder as I Wander." He got her to repeat it eight times, paying her twenty-five cents for each rendition, while he scribbled down the words and melody.

Niles later added some additional verses of his own and sang it during his concerts. He recorded it in 1958 and it has since become immensely popular.

He never saw the girl again and all his efforts over the years never unearthed the original source of the song. Niles died in 1980.

Sounds from Space

Christmas made it into space for the first time in 1965. Astronauts Tom Stafford and Wally Schirra were orbiting on board Gemini 6 a few days before Christmas when they contacted Mission Control to report an unusual sighting.

"We have an object, looks like a satellite going from north to south, probably in polar orbit," Stafford, who was the Gemini pilot, said. "I see a command module and eight smaller modules in front. The pilot of the command module is wearing a red suit …."

The pair then pulled out a harmonica and a set of sleigh bells and proceeded to give the world its first space carol.

While we are on the subject of "Jingle Bells," there is a verse to the song that is hardly ever sung and that few people know. We came across it in Wikipedia. The lyrics are as follows:

A day or two ago,
The story I must tell
I went out on the snow,
And on my back I fell;
A gent was riding by
In a one-horse open sleigh,
He laughed as there I sprawling laid,
But quickly drove away.

Carols from
Around the World

We're all familiar with the standard songbook of carols from England and America. And most of us know a few traditional carols from France and Germany that have been translated and popularized in North America. But what about carols from the rest of the world? Have you ever wondered what they're singing in Norway on Christmas Day? Or whether Australians dream of a "White Christmas" in a holiday season that comes at the beginning of their summer?

Christmas is celebrated in every part of the world where Christians live—whether the celebrations are small and private or observed as a national holiday. And for the many different countries that observe the holiday, there are just as many different carols and carolling traditions—unknown to most of us in the United States and Canada but equally as beautiful or as imaginative as the carols we sing, and certainly deserving of mention in this book.

From Spain to Sweden and from Puerto Rico to the Philippines, join us on a trip around the world as we look at some familiar and many not-so-familiar Christmas songs from every corner of the globe.

Brainteaser Trivia

(Answers on page 218)

Pumpkin Pies

1. Who is Santa Claus, according to the lyrics of the Irish holiday song "Christmas in Killarney"?

    a. One of the boys from home

    b. A fat man from Dublin

    c. A jolly old elf

    d. A guest in a green suit

2. Which famous Canadian singer/songwriter dreams of spending the holidays in Jamaica, in the lyrics to the song "Reggae Christmas"?

    a. Alanis Morissette

    b. Nelly Furtado

    c. Leonard Cohen

    d. Bryan Adams

3. "Staffan var en Stalledrang" is a Swedish Christmas song about a saint whose feast day falls on December 26. Name the saint.

    a. St. Stephen

    b. St. Nicholas

    c. St. Peter

    d. St. Francis

4. In the third verse of "Once in Royal David's City," all Christian children are told to follow Christ's example by being what?

   a. Cheerful, happy, laughing
   b. Mild, obedient, good
   c. Trustworthy, helpful, kind
   d. Respectful, docile, silent

5. "Tu Scendi Dalle Stelle," a popular nineteenth century Italian carol, literally translates to "you came down from ..." where?

   a. Above   b. The stars   c. Heaven   d. The sky

6. What is the city that is referred to in the nineteenth century Irish Christmas carol "Once in Royal David's City"?

   a. Nazareth   b. Bethlehem   c. Jerusalem   d. Jericho

7. Which Canadian carol is also known by the name of "Jesous Ahatonhia"?

   a. "The Huron Carol"   c. "The Algonquin Carol"
   b. "The Iroquois Carol"   d. "The Ojibwa Carol"

8. Instead of "Auld Lang Syne," what other famous music is heard in Vienna, Austria, on New Year's Eve?

   a. "The Blue Danube Waltz"   c. "Ode to Joy"
   b. "Eine Kleine Nachtmusik"   d. "The Hallelujah Chorus"

9. In Puerto Rico, Christmas carollers visit homes and demand (through the lyrics of their songs) to be let in. This custom is known as *asalto,* which translates in English to what?

a. Open the door   c. Knock knock

b. Home invasion   d. Celebration

10. By what other name is the traditional Irish carol "Curoo Curoo" also known?

a. "Carol of the Saints"   c. "Carol of the Birds"

b. "Carol of the Innocents"   d. "Carol of the Shepherds"

11. The Australian Christmas carol "Six White Boomers" depicts a group of which indigenous animal pulling Santa's sleigh?

a. Koala bears   b. Dingos   c. Kangaroos   d. Emus

12. In Portugal, carols called the *Janeiras* are sung in the streets at Christmastime. These carols all share which common theme?

a. The new year   c. Baby Jesus

b. John the Baptist   d. The yule log

13. Originally written in the Scots language, the literal translation of "Auld Lang Syne" is what?

a. "Old Long Since"   c. "Old Eyes of Mine"

b. "Days Gone By"   d. "Happy New Year"

14. What is the Spanish word for *Christmas carol*?

    a. Villancico   b. Navidano   c. Christaria   d. Musica

15. "Trei Pastori" is a beloved Romanian Christmas carol. What does it mean in English?

    a. "Three Shepherds"   c. "Three Stories"
    b. "Three Wise Men"   d. "Three Miracles"

16. "Gesu Bambino" was written by Italian-American Pietro A. Yon, famous for his compositions for which instrument?

    a. Piano   b. Harp   c. Cello   d. Organ

17. The Dutch carol "Sinterklaas, Goed Heilig Man" sings of which revered Christmas figure?

    a. Rudolph   b. Baby Jesus   c. St. Nicholas   d. Jack Frost

18. In which country would you most likely find yourself singing the Christmas song "Pasko Na Naman" in Tagalog?

    a. The Netherlands   c. The United States
    b. The Philippines   d. New Zealand

19. Name the popular Disney tune that has been adapted as a Christmas song in Sweden, Norway, and Denmark.

    a. "Someday My Prince Will Come"
    b. "Can You Feel the Love Tonight?"
    c. "When You Wish Upon a Star"
    d. "Baby Mine"

20. Who or what is the Gitchi-Manitou that is sung about in "The Huron Carol"?

    a. A star   b. A baby   c. A manger   d. God

21. "Baloo, Lammy" ("Lullabye, Little Lamb") is a seventeenth century traditional carol that originated in what country?

    a. Canada   b. Germany   c. Scotland   d. Ireland

22. Puerto Rican singer/songwriter Jose Feliciano wrote the well-known Christmas pop song "Feliz Navidad" in 1970. What affliction was Feliciano born with?

    a. Blindness   b. Deafness   c. Diabetes   d. Cleft palate

23. "Jesus' Bloemhof" ("The Garden of Jesus") is a fifteenth century carol originating in which European country?

    a. Switzerland   c. Luxembourg
    b. Belgium   d. The Netherlands

24. "Dormi, Dormi Bambino," which is featured on the album *The Three Tenors Christmas,* is a traditional song from which country?

    a. Germany   b. Spain   c. Italy   d. Switzerland

Plum Puddings

25. In Austria, what object might you find carollers carrying around from house to house on Christmas Eve?

    a. A large present   c. A Christmas cake
    b. A small fir tree   d. A manger

26. The traditional Italian carol "Canzone d'i Zampognari" is known by what name in English?

    a. "Carol of the Harpists"   c. "Carol of the Bagpipers"
    b. "Carol of the Cellists"   d. "Carol of the Drummers"

27. Which famous Dane wrote the lyrics to the nineteenth century carol "Barn Jesus" ("Child Jesus")?

    a. Karen Blixen   c. Hans Christian Andersen
    b. Søren Kierkegaard   d. Niels Bohr

28. "De Nederige Geboorte" ("The Simple Birth") is known in English by another name indicative of its origins. What is it?

    a. "The Basque Carol"   c. "The Prussian Carol"
    b. "The Sicilian Carol"   d. "The Flemish Carol"

29. "Fum, Fum, Fum" is one of the most popular Christmas carols originating from which European country?

    a. Spain   b. Portugal   c. Italy   d. Greece

30. The Italian carol "Gesu Bambino" recalls which legend centring around Christ's birth?

    a. Legend of the Three Wise Men
    b. Legend of the Talking Animals
    c. Legend of Flowers Blooming
    d. Legend of the Holly Wreath

31. Due to its northern geography, what is traditionally the most common theme in Swedish Christmas songs?

    a. Mittens   b. Snow   c. Candles   d. Reindeer

32. On which two types of occasions would you probably hear "Auld Lang Syne" played in Taiwan?

   a. Baptisms and birthday parties
   b. Funerals and graduations
   c. Family reunions and elections
   d. Weddings and baby showers

33. Carols by candlelight is a twentieth century custom involving large groups of people gathering together in the weeks leading up to Christmas to sing carols by, as the name implies, candlelight. In which country did this custom originate?

   a. Sweden   b. South Africa   c. Australia   d. Canada

34. The original version of the Ukrainian "Carol of the Bells" tells the tale of a bird bringing tidings of the year to come. What type of bird was it?

   a. Swallow   b. Nightingale   c. Dove   d. Partridge

35. *Parang* bands move from house to house serenading people with Christmas music in which Caribbean country?

   a. Cuba   c. Trinidad and Tobago
   b. Jamaica   d. St. Martin

36. Complete the following verse from the Irish carol "Come Buy My Nice Fresh Ivy":

> Ah, won't you buy my ivy?
> It's the loveliest I've seen.
> Ah, won't you buy my holly?

a. Oh you who love the green   c. And crown an Irish queen

b. And give it to Kathleen   d. And bless the fair Christine

37. "The Huron Carol" was the first Canadian Christmas carol. In what year was it written?

a. 1641   b. 1741   c. 1841   d. 1941

38. Traditional Christmas carols from Venezuela are called *aguinaldos*. In English, what does this word mean?

a. Song   b. Birth   c. Joy   d. Gift

39. The lyrics of the popular carol "The Three Drovers" tell of a hot, dry, and summery Christmas night. From which country does this carol originate?

a. New Zealand   c. South Africa

b. Australia   d. Argentina

40. Instead of swaddling clothes, what wraps the Baby Jesus in Canada's "The Huron Carol"?

a. Birch bark   b. Leaves   c. Rabbit skin   d. Moonlight

41. Which European country's Christmas tradition had people dressing up as manger characters and travelling door to door singing *kolyadki* (carols)?

a. Poland   b. Hungary   c. Romania   d. Russia

42. The lyrics of the song "Christmas on the Beach" urge the rejection of traditional wintry holiday things such as holly, mistletoe, reindeer, and Christmas trees. From which country does this song originate?

a. Brazil   b. Australia   c. New Zealand   d. Barbados

43. The title character in the song "Rudolph the Red-Nosed Reindeer" is known as "Petteri Punakuono" in which Scandinavian country?

a. Denmark   b. Finland   c. Norway   d. Sweden

44. In the ancient Welsh Christmas custom of the *Mari Lwyd* ("Blessed Mary"), a group of men would travel from door to door singing and rhyming and carrying which of the following objects raised up on a pole?

a. A skein   b. A skunk   c. A skull   d. A skillet

45. The traditional Czech carol "Hajej, nynej Jezisku" was popularized in its English version, "The Rocking Carol," by which well-known singer?

a. Barbra Streisand   c. Whitney Houston

b. Céline Dion   d. Julie Andrews

46. Name the seventy-five-year-old Asian musical theatre group that puts on a series of Christmas carol concerts every year.

a. The Hong Kong Singers   c. The Pakistani Performers

b. The Philippine Songbirds   d. The Cambodian Choir

47. Until 1948, the melody of which holiday song was used as the South Korean national anthem?

a. "The First Nowell"   c. "Auld Lang Syne"

b. "Jingle Bells"   d. "Little Drummer Boy"

Chestnuts

48. Which nineteenth century carol composer who was born in Dublin, Ireland, wrote anti-Fenian hymns for the Protestant Orange Order?

a. Sarah Flower Adams   c. Mrs. Cecil Frances Alexander

b. Frances Ridley Havergal   d. Elizabeth Barrett Browning

49. "Vamos Pastoricitos" ("Let Us Go, O Shepherds") is a Christmas carol originating from which South American country?

a. Colombia   b. Peru   c. Chile   d. Argentina

50. What small object might you find Greek Christmas carollers holding as they travel from door to door?

a. A wooden donkey   c. A wooden star
b. A wooden ship   d. A loaf of freshly baked bread

51. What was the original name for the music of the Irish carol "Come Buy My Nice Fresh Ivy"?

a. "Patrick's Song"   c. "Irishmen Rejoice"
b. "O'Carolan's Lament"   d. "Hymn of Callaghan"

52. "Carol of the Bells" was adapted from a folk song from which Eastern European country?

a. Romania   c. Poland
b. Czech Republic   d. Ukraine

53. "God Is Born" ("Bog sie Rodzi") is the national Christmas hymn of which Eastern European country?

a. Albania   b. Bulgaria   c. Transylvania   d. Poland

54. What carol was written by a Scottish-born newspaper editor who was a strong agitator for Irish independence?
    a. "God Rest Ye Merry, Gentlemen"
    b. "We Wish You a Merry Christmas"
    c. "Angels from the Realms of Glory"
    d. "Joy to the World"

55. In its original Ukrainian, "Carol of the Bells" is known as "Shchedryk." What does it mean?
    a. Pious   b. Pure   c. Bountiful   d. Holy

56. Instead of a partridge in a pear tree, what would you find in the New Zealand version of "The Twelve Days of Christmas"?
    a. A moa in a mamaku tree   c. A kiwi in a kapuka tree
    b. A pukeko in a ponga tree   d. An albatross in an akeake tree

57. "Nu Sa Kommer Julen" ("Now Christmas Is Coming") is a favourite Christmas hymn from which northern country?
    a. Iceland   b. Scotland   c. Canada   d. Sweden

58. How does the Welsh carol "Canu Cwnsela" translate in English?
    a. "Christ Child"   c. "Shepherd's Crook"
    b. "Christmas Chimes"   d. "Wassail Song"

59. In which country might you find carollers known as *Sternsinger* (star singers) parading about at Christmastime?

a. Norway   b. Switzerland   c. Croatia   d. Greenland

60. "Te Harinui," or "Great Joy," is a Christmas carol commemorating the first official Christian service in New Zealand on Christmas Day of what year?

a. 1614   b. 1714   c. 1814   d. 1914

61. *Klopfelngehen* was an old German Christmas tradition where groups of needy people would go from house to house singing hymns in exchange for food. The term literally means what?

a. Charity   b. Knocking   c. Carolling   d. Kindness

62. The Caribbean carol "The Virgin Mary Had a Baby Boy" is played to a calypso beat. What country is it from?

a. Jamaica   c. Trinidad and Tobago
b. Barbados   d. The Bahamas

63. In 1996, a Finnish classically trained rock band called *Apocalyptica* recorded a version of "The Little Drummer Boy" arranged for which instrument?

a. Piano   b. Violin   c. Flute   d. Cello

64. In Slovakian Christmas tradition, men and boys dress up as angels and shepherds and visit nearby homes singing and re-enacting the nativity. They are called *Jaslickari*, which means what?

a. Surprise guests   c. Messengers of Jesus

b. Bethlehem carollers   d. Night elves

65. The Irish composer of "Once in Royal David's City" also wrote many other hymns that are still popular today. Which of the following is *not* one of her compositions?

a. "All Things Bright and Beautiful"

b. "There Is a Green Hill Far Away"

c. "Nearer, My God, to Thee"

d. "Jesus Calls Us"

66. "Los Peces en el Río" is one of Spain's most popular Christmas carols. Its lyrics sing of the Virgin Mary going about everyday tasks. Which of the following tasks is *not* part of the carol?

a. Combing her hair   c. Cooking breakfast

b. Washing diapers   d. Washing her hands

67. The traditional Catalonian carol "El Cant dels Ocells" ("Song of the Birds") tells of birds announcing the birth of Jesus to the world through their joyous song. According to the carol, which bird flew to Bethlehem to greet the baby personally and serenade him with a song of love?

a. A partridge   b. A dove   c. A lark   d. A cardinal

68. The words to the carol "Once in Royal David's City" were originally written as a poem by Mrs. Cecil Frances Alexander for whom?

a. Her daughter
b. Her husband, an Anglican bishop
c. Her mother
d. Her godchildren

69. Who was the Irish-born carol writer who translated a Latin poem on the subject of syphilis into English?

a. Nahum Tate
b. Nicholas Brady
c. Mrs. Cecil Frances Alexander
d. William Devereux

70. What honour was bestowed by English monarchs William and Mary on the Irish-born author of "While Shepherds Watched Their Flocks by Night"?

    a. Knighthood

    b. Naming as poet laureate

    c. Dukedom

    d. Naming as governor-general

71. What is the more commonly used title for the carol "Song of the Angels at the Nativity of our Blessed Saviour," which was written by a native of Dublin?

    a. "Angels We Have Heard on High"

    b. "The First Nowell"

    c. "While Shepherds Watched Their Flocks by Night"

    d. "Angels from the Realms of Glory"

Did You Know?

Rewriting Shakespeare

A writer would have to be very smart, very conceited, very stupid, or some combination of all three to undertake the rewriting of the plays of William Shakespeare. Nahum Tate (born Teate) clearly was not stupid since he was named as poet laureate of England in 1692. So we are left to assume he was both smart and conceited—as well as being somewhat of a royal toady.

Tate, an Irish Protestant, was born in Dublin in 1652 and graduated from Trinity College twenty years later. It didn't take him long after that to decide that his future lay not in Ireland's rainy capital but in the glamorous theatrical world of London, where Charles II, who earned the nickname "The Merry Monarch" for his hedonistic (some might say debauched) lifestyle, had recently been restored to the throne.

England was still deeply divided along religious and political lines following Charles's restoration and Tate apparently felt that Shakespeare's classic play *Richard II* did not show proper respect for the monarchy. Accordingly, he took it upon himself not only to change the text but even to alter the names of the characters so that, in his words, every scene was "full of respect to Majesty and the dignity of courts."

As if bowdlerizing *Richard II* wasn't enough, Tate decided that he didn't like the ending to *King Lear* and modified it to add a marriage between Cornelia and Edgar. Shakespeare must have rolled over in his grave!

Perhaps in part because of his tinkering with the Bard, Tate never seemed to earn the respect of his peers. When he was named poet laureate by William and Mary after the death of Charles II, a far greater contemporary, Alexander Pope, was sharply critical of the appointment and attacked Tate's poems in *The Dunciad*.

Nahum Tate would probably have become a mere footnote to the history of the Restoration were it not for one single literary contribution: although some scholars dispute it, he appears to have written the words for the immensely popular carol "While Shepherds Watched Their Flocks by Night." First published in 1696 in *New Version of the Psalms of David,* co-authored with fellow Irishman Nicholas Brady, the text soon became the only Christmas carol recognized by the Anglican Church for inclusion in its services. Over the centuries, it has been sung to many tunes, to the point where *The New Oxford Book of Carols* offers no fewer than seven different musical versions.

Sadly, Tate's life did not have a happy ending. He died in London in 1715, having spent his final years living in poverty and pursued by creditors.

Christmas Carols Down Under

Australian singer/songwriter Rolf Harris has had a long and rather eclectic career. He sang with the Beatles and was commissioned to paint an official portrait of Queen Elizabeth II. He invented a homemade instrument called the wobbleboard, which he has used in many of his recordings, most notably "Tie Me Kangaroo Down, Sport," which became an international hit in the 1960s and was performed at the opening ceremony of the 1982 Commonwealth Games in Brisbane.

It was also in the 1960s that Harris and his friend John D. Brown discussed the absurdity of singing traditional wintry Christmas songs while living in Australia where the Christmas season falls at the beginning of summer.

Together the pair wrote a song more appropriate to the warm climate of Australia. "Six White Boomers" tells of an overheating Santa Claus reuniting a young kangaroo with his mother (boomers are large kangaroos, named for the sound they make as they hit the ground while jumping).

This song is one of many Christmas tunes that celebrate the uniqueness of the Christmas season down under. Other Australian carols include "Aussie Jingle Bells" (instead of snow, the lyrics sing of dashing through the bush), "Let Us Barbeque," "The Three Drovers," and "Aussie Twelve Days of Christmas," which replaces the traditional partridge in a pear tree with a kookaburra (or, in some variations, an emu) in a gum tree.

The Mighty Gitchi-Manitou

Also known as "Twas in the Moon of Wintertime," "The Huron Carol" is the earliest known carol ever written in the Americas. It also holds the distinction of being the most famous carol ever translated from a Native American tongue.

The carol was created in 1641 by French Jesuit missionary Jean de Brebeuf for the Huron people in a region of what is now the province of Ontario. Written in the native language of the Hurons, Father Brebeuf used the music from a sixteenth century French folk song and called his carol "Jesous Ahatonhia" ("Jesus, He Is Born"). With his lyrics, Brebeuf retells the story of the nativity by replacing biblical images with ones that would have been more familiar to the Huron people. Thus, instead of a stable, the Baby Jesus is found in a lodge of "broken bark" and wrapped in rabbit skin rather than swaddling clothes. Shepherds are replaced with hunters and the Three Wise Men are represented as chiefs bearing gifts of fur skins for the baby in the place of gold, frankincense, and myrrh.

Unfortunately, Father Brebeuf died a violent death at the hands of an invading Iroquois tribe. But his carol remained preserved orally by generations of Hurons until the eighteenth century, when it was heard, written down, and thereby saved by another Jesuit priest, Father Villeneuve.

In 1926, "Jesous Ahatonhia" was translated into the English version we are now familiar with. The carol is known around the world, but holds a very special place in the hearts of Canadians.

Classical Carols

Determining what Christmas music qualifies as *classical* is obviously an arbitrary decision. Who are we to say that "O Come All Ye Faithful" or "Joy to the World," for example, are not classic hymns?

Yet there is a genre of Christmas music that does not fit comfortably into the category of *carols*. These are works by some of the world's greatest composers that were written in the form of oratorios, ballets, cantatas, etc.

Many of the great composers tried their hand at Christmas music at one time or another. The distinguished list includes George Frideric Handel, Johann Sebastian Bach, Wolfgang Amadeus Mozart, Franz Schubert, Hector Berlioz, Ludwig van Beethoven, Pyotr Ilyich Tchaikovsky, Felix Mendelssohn, Camille Saint-Saëns, Marc-Antoine Charpentier, Frederic Chopin, Ralph Vaughan Williams, and Benjamin Britten.

Unfortunately, except for favourites like Handel's "Hallelujah Chorus" from the *Messiah* and Tchaikovsky's *The Nutcracker,* many of these wonderful works of music are unknown to most people. Here's an opportunity to learn more about them. Perhaps you and your family will be intrigued enough to buy some new Christmas CDs or attend a holiday concert.

Brainteaser Trivia

(Answers on page 220)

Pumpkin Pies

1. Which famous composer wrote the classical masterpiece *Christmas Oratorio* in 1734?

   a. Beethoven   b. Brahms   c. Bach   d. Mozart

2. Handel's *Messiah* was originally written and performed for which Christian holy day?

   a. Christmas   b. Easter   c. Good Friday   d. Ash Wednesday

3. Which famous Russian composer wrote the music for the 1892 Christmas ballet *The Nutcracker*?

   a. Rimsky-Korsakov   c. Rachmaninoff
   b. Stravinsky   d. Tchaikovsky

4. Which of the following is *not* the name of a musical number from the Christmas ballet *The Nutcracker*?

   a. "Waltz of the Flowers"   c. "Dance of the Dollies"
   b. "Waltz of the Snowflakes"   d. "Dance of the Sugar-Plum Fairy"

5. Where was George Frideric Handel, composer of the *Messiah,* born?

    a. England   b. Ireland   c. Luxembourg   d. Germany

6. In what century was *A Ceremony of Carols* written by Benjamin Britten?

    a. Eighteenth   b. Nineteenth   c. Twentieth   d. Twenty-first

7. The great German composer Johann Strauss wrote a polka entitled "Donner und Blitzen," but it wasn't named after Santa's reindeer. What is the German translation of the words?

    a. Hope and glory   c. Love and hate

    b. Peace and war   d. Thunder and lightning

8. The composer of "Ave Maria" also left behind an "Unfinished Symphony." Who was he?

    a. Johann Strauss   c. Johann Sebastian Bach

    b. Franz Schubert   d. Joseph Haydn

9. During what period is Handel's *Messiah* most commonly performed?

    a. Lent   b. Holy Week   c. Advent   d. Pentecost

10. Of what nationality was Hector Berlioz, who wrote *L'enfance du Christ*?

   a. German   b. Swiss   c. French   d. Belgian

11. Apart from his *Messiah,* what other work is Handel best known for?

   a. *Water Music*   c. *The Four Seasons*
   b. *1812 Overture*   d. *Sinfonia*

Plum Puddings

12. To which family members did Hector Berlioz dedicate Part I of his Christmas masterpiece, *L'Enfance du Christ*?

   a. His parents   c. His godchildren
   b. His brothers   d. His nieces

13. In which European city was Handel's *Messiah* first performed?

   a. London   b. Berlin   c. Vienna   d. Dublin

14. Charles Jennens, who provided the concept for the *Messiah,* expected that Handel would require a year to complete the oratorio. How long did it actually take him?

   a. Twenty-four days   c. Ten years
   b. Two years   d. Twenty-two years

15. Benjamin Britten's *A Ceremony of Carols* was composed during a voyage between which two countries?

    a. India and Australia

    c. The United States and England

    b. France and Canada

    d. Scotland and Spain

16. Which popular nineteenth century carol did German classical composer Felix Mendelssohn provide the music for?

    a. "Silent Night"

    b. "Hark! The Herald Angels Sing"

    c. "Joy to the World"

    d. "Away in a Manger"

17. Which English king is said to have created a tradition that continues to this day when he stood upon hearing his first performance of the "Hallelujah Chorus"?

    a. Henry VIII

    c. George II

    b. Charles II

    d. William of Orange

18. The *Messiah* is written in what musical style?

    a. Baroque   b. Classical   c. Romantic   d. Renaissance

19. What great poet and novelist is generally credited with the lyrics of the classic Christmas favourite "Ave Maria"?

    a. Charles Dickens

    c. Henry James

    b. Sir Walter Scott

    d. William Makepeace Thackeray

20. What aria from Handel's *Messiah* is frequently sung at church funerals?

   a. "The Old Rugged Cross"
   b. "I Know That My Redeemer Liveth"
   c. "Abide with Me"
   d. "All Things Bright and Beautiful"

21. From which book of the New Testament are the lyrics for the "Hallelujah Chorus" drawn?

   a. Matthew   b. Acts   c. Revelation   d. Romans

22. Bach's *Christmas Oratorio* consists of six what?

   a. Tone poems   b. Sonatas   c. Cantatas   d. Symphonies

23. Camille Saint-Saëns was French but he wrote his *Christmas Oratorio* in another language. What was it?

   a. Latin   b. Hebrew   c. Greek   d. Aramaic

24. The British composer Ralph Vaughan Williams wrote a ballet entitled *On Christmas Night* that was based on which literary work?

   a. *The Gift of the Magi*
   b. *A Christmas Carol*
   c. *A Visit from St. Nicholas*
   d. *The Pickwick Papers*

Chestnuts

25. Which newly invented instrument was composer Pyotr Ilyich Tchaikovsky eager to use in his Christmas ballet *The Nutcracker* because of its "heavenly sweet sound"?

    a. Oboe   b. Xylophone   c. Harp   d. Celesta

26. Benjamin Britten's Christmas choral piece *A Boy Was Born* was written in 1934 for which British musical organization?

    a. The London Symphony Orchestra
    b. The Royal Philharmonic Orchestra
    c. The Morriston Orpheus Choir
    d. The BBC Singers

27. Hector Berlioz wrote in his *Memoirs* that his Christmas composition *L'Enfance du Christ* was influenced by his "first musical impression." What was it?

    a. His baptism   c. His wedding
    b. His first communion   d. His mother's funeral

28. *Sonatina in Diem Nativitatus Christi MCMXVIII* by Ferruccio Busoni was dedicated to his son Benvenuto who had enlisted to fight in which major war?

    a. Franco-Prussian War   c. Second World War
    b. First World War   d. Korean War

29. Which French composer wrote the seventeenth century Christmas masterpiece *Messe de minuit pour Noël*?

   a. Claude Debussy
   b. Georges Bizet
   c. Leo Delibes
   d. Marc-Antoine Charpentier

30. In 1814, Ludwig van Beethoven published an arrangement of a well-known Christmas carol for piano, violin, cello, and three voices. Which carol was it?

   a. "O Tannenbaum"
   b. "O Come, O Come, Emmanuel"
   c. "O Holy Night"
   d. "O Sanctissima"

31. Ralph Vaughan Williams, perhaps England's greatest twentieth century composer, wrote a Christmas cantata in 1953–54 that has been performed on PBS by the Mormon Tabernacle Choir. What is its name?

   a. *Hodie*
   b. *Toward the Unknown Region*
   c. *Magnificat*
   d. *Festival Te Deum*

32. How old was Ralph Vaughan Williams when he finished his Christmas cantata?

   a. Nineteen
   b. Twenty-six
   c. Eighty-two
   d. Ninety-seven

33. The traditional Polish Christmas carol "Lulajze Jezuniu" ("Lullabye to Jesus") was adapted by which famous composer for his "Scherzo in B Minor"?

a. Chopin   b. Mozart   c. Beethoven   d. Bach

34. Which great composer wrote a new arrangement of Handel's *Messiah* that was first performed in Vienna in 1789?

a. Bach   b. Mozart   c. Beethoven   d. Johann Strauss

35. Over how many days was Bach's *Christmas Oratorio* originally meant to be performed?

a. Three   b. Six   c. Ten   d. Twelve

36. Who wrote the now seldom performed *Oratorio de Noël* in 1858?

a. Georges Bizet   c. Hector Berlioz
b. Camille Saint-Saëns   d. Georges Offenbach

37. Which Richard Strauss composition is included on *The Three Tenors Christmas*?

a. "Ein Heldenleben"   c. "Friedenstag"
b. "Festive Prelude"   d. "Wiegenlied"

38. What classic English-language poem was the source for the Latin lyrics of "Ave Maria"?
    a. "Ode to a Nightingale"   c. "To a Skylark"
    b. "The Faerie Queene"   d. "The Lady of the Lake"

39. How old was Franz Schubert when he wrote "Ave Maria"?
    a. Fifteen   c. Thirty-one
    b. Twenty-eight   d. Forty-six

40. When Franz Schubert died in 1828, he was buried alongside what great composer?
    a. Bach   b. Mozart   c. Handel   d. Beethoven

41. The first section of the *Messiah* draws heavily from which book of the Old Testament?
    a. Psalms   b. Proverbs   c. Job   d. Isaiah

42. In what language is *A Ceremony of Carols* mainly written?
    a. Welsh   c. Gaelic
    b. Norman French   d. Old English

43. The ending of Greg Lake's "I Believe in Father Christmas" was inspired by a suite by which famous Russian composer?
    a. Tchaikovsky   c. Prokofiev
    b. Stravinsky   d. Rimsky-Korsakov

Did You Know?

The Strauss Controversy

Richard Strauss is not particularly remembered as a composer of Christmas music; in fact, he is most often associated in people's minds with the haunting opening theme music of *2001: A Space Odyssey.* But some of his works have been performed in conjunction with the holidays, and his classic lullaby "Wiegenlied" ("Träume, träume, du mein süsses Leben") is included on the wonderful *The Three Tenors Christmas* album.

Strauss has always been a controversial figure, both during his lifetime and since his death in 1949. Musicians and critics have disputed the quality of his work, and Strauss seemed to agree with his detractors, describing himself toward the end of his life, perhaps ironically, as a "first-class second-rate composer."

However, his politics were even more controversial than his musical capabilities. Strauss was accused by some of being a Nazi collaborator after being appointed head of the State Music Bureau by Joseph Goebbels in 1933. Although he claimed he was never a party member, Strauss became friendly with many high-ranking Nazis and composed the anthem that was performed at the opening ceremonies of the 1936 Berlin Olympics, with Adolf Hitler in attendance.

Strauss's defenders claimed that he only accepted the position in the hope that he might be able to protect his Jewish daughter-in-law (which he did when she and his son were arrested some years later). He resigned the position as a result of a dispute—and a subsequent Gestapo investigation—over including the name of a Jewish librettist on the playbill and posters of the premiere of one of his operas.

After the war ended, he was investigated by the Allies for collaboration with the Hitler regime but was cleared of all charges in 1948, shortly before he died.

A Classical Bonding

The lyrics to "Ave Maria" are based on a Latin prayer that dates back to the earliest days of the Christian church. Over the centuries, many authors, including Shakespeare, have included adaptations of the prayer in their writings. However, it was apparently the version contained in the German translation of Sir Walter Scott's "The Lady of the Lake" that was the inspiration for Franz Schubert to compose the timeless classic that has become a standard during the Christmas season. Here are the English words, which few people know:

> Ave Maria! Ave Maria! maiden mild!
> Listen to a maiden's prayer!
> Thou canst hear though from the wild,
> Thou canst save amid despair.

Safe may we sleep beneath thy care,
Though banish'd, outcast and reviled—
Maiden! hear a maiden's prayer;
Mother, hear a suppliant child!
Ave Maria!

Ave Maria! undefiled!
The flinty couch we now must share
Shall seem this down of eider piled,
If thy protection hover there.
The murky cavern's heavy air
Shall breathe of balm if thou hast smiled;
Then, Maiden! hear a maiden's prayer;
Mother, list a suppliant child!
Ave Maria!

Ave Maria! stainless styled!
Foul demons of the earth and air,
From this their wonted haunt exiled,
Shall flee before thy presence fair.
We bow us to our lot of care,
Beneath thy guidance reconciled;
Hear for a maid a maiden's prayer,
And for a father hear a child!
Ave Maria!

The soaring melody is perhaps Schubert's best remembered work, although he penned a number of symphonies (including the famous "Unfinished Symphony"), sonatas, rondeaus, and other melodies. What makes all this especially remarkable is that he lived most of his life in poverty, suffered from a venereal disease, and died at the tender age of thirty-one.

Schubert's career was remarkable considering that he was born into a family that was not particularly skilled in music and had very little early training in the art. It was only after he came to the attention of Antonio Salieri that Schubert began to blossom. (Salieri was Mozart's lifelong rival and was accused by some of murdering him out of jealousy. The story was retold in the movie *Amadeus*.)

Under Salieri's tutelage, Schubert began composing while he was in his mid-teens and turned out an amazing number of works (over seven hundred) before his untimely death in 1828. This volume of work was made possible only by financial support from wealthy patrons; without this aid Schubert might have spent his life as an undistinguished teacher in a school run by his father. His compositions failed to generate any income in his early years and he was entirely dependent on the generosity of others to survive.

His lifestyle was free-wheeling (some historians refer to it as "bohemian"). He loved a good party and to hang out with his buddies at the Red Hedgehog tavern. The Red Hedgehog was Vienna's social centre for musicians and was frequented in later years by Johannes Brahms.

Schubert's physical stature was unprepossessing. He was barely over five feet tall and, to put it politely, roly-poly in body, thus earning him the nickname Little Mushroom. However, this didn't prevent him from attracting the ladies and by the age of twenty-five he had contracted syphilis, which is believed to have contributed to his death (although the official cause was typhoid). He tried to marry once but the application was rejected by the Roman Catholic Church on the grounds of Schubert's poverty.

"Ave Maria" was written in 1825, less than three years before Schubert's death, as a simple rendition for voice and piano. The composer appears to have regarded the hymn as the culminating work of his career, writing later to his parents: "My audience expressed great delight at the solemnity of my Hymn to the Blessed Virgin; it seems to have infected the minds of listeners. I believe I have attained this result by never forcing on myself religious ecstasy, and never setting myself to compose such hymns or prayers except when I am involuntarily overcome by the feeling and spirit of devotion, in that case devotion is usually of the right and genuine kind."

Those words tell us a lot about the man. He was not deeply pious (as his lifestyle attests) but was prone to episodes of religious fervour, one of which led to the composition of one of the most reverent and beautiful hymns of all time. It stands as a fitting epitaph to him.

Standing for "Hallelujah"

First-time attendees at a performance of Handel's *Messiah* are often startled when the audience members rise *en masse* at the start of the "Hallelujah Chorus" and remain on their feet until the rousing hymn of praise is finished. No other classical work inspires this kind of respect, so what is it that makes "Hallelujah" so special?

In fact, the tradition dates back over two hundred fifty years to 1742, the year *Messiah* debuted to the public as an Easter spectacular in Dublin, Ireland. (George Frideric Handel had actually composed it the previous summer in an incredible twenty-four days.)

Although the oratorio was what we would today call a *smash hit* in Ireland, it was a few months later in London that the tradition of standing appears to have begun. Although some scholars dispute the origin, the generally accepted story is that it happened during the debut performance in the English capital when the reigning monarch, George II, was in attendance. The king, it is said, was so moved by the inspiring opening strains of the "Hallelujah Chorus" that he leaped to his feet in enthusiasm. In those days, everyone followed a monarch's lead, and so, seeing this, the rest of the audience immediately rose as well and the tradition was established.

Over the years, some people have questioned whether it was indeed Handel's music that prompted the king to rise or something much more mundane—perhaps he simply needed to go to the bathroom or stretch his legs. It has even been suggested that the king had been told that the "Hallelujah Chorus" marked the end of Part II of the oratorio and had risen in preparation for leaving the theatre. Whatever the truth, the custom continues to this day in the English-speaking world, although it is seldom observed elsewhere.

The story of how George Frideric Handel (*Frideric* was his preferred spelling for his middle name) came to write *Messiah* is remarkable. Like many composers of the era, he was chronically short of money and depended on the beneficence of others to survive. In this case, his patron was the Duke of Devonshire, the Lord Lieutenant of Ireland, who invited a sick and depressed Handel to come to Dublin in the summer of 1741 to conduct a series of charitable concerts. At about the same time, Handel received an idea for an oratorio based on the life of Jesus, from a man named Charles Jennens who dabbled at music (and a lot of other things) but lacked the skill to bring his concept to reality.

At that point, Handel was at the nadir of his life and career, so he seized upon the duke's invitation immediately and made the journey from London to Dublin. Enthralled with Jennens' idea, he immediately set to work on what was to be his masterwork, completing it in an astounding twenty-four days (some sources say twenty-one).

In an interesting footnote, another towering figure of the era, Jonathan Swift, blocked the initial performance of *Messiah* at St. Patrick's Cathedral, where he was dean, insisting that it be renamed *A Sacred Oratorio* and that profits from any concert be given to charities of his choice.

Handel died in 1759 and is buried in Westminster Abbey.

A Perilous Voyage

The year was 1942. Continental Europe had been overrun by the Nazis. The United States had just entered the Second World War and the North Atlantic was swarming with U-boats seeking to cripple the supply lines between North America and Britain.

The great composer Benjamin Britten had left his native England for the United States in 1939, shortly before the European phase of the war began. It has been suggested that his action was motivated by the fact that he was a pacifist and the United States was following a policy of neutrality toward the looming hostilities. However, other sources contend that the journey to America was motivated more by his disenchantment with the musical establishment in England.

Whatever the reason, by 1942 Britten had decided it was time to return home. But the decision was easier than its execution. All civilian passenger traffic between the United States and Britain had ended. The great pre-war ocean liners had been pressed into service as troop carriers. Merchant ships crossed the North Atlantic in large convoys escorted by fleets of destroyers and frigates, but even with that protection casualties were high as deadly and efficient U-boats were able to penetrate the security shields.

Britten finally managed to book passage aboard a Swedish cargo ship, the *Axel Johnson,* in April 1942. His on-board accommodations were anything but elegant—his cabin was right next to the ship's refrigeration plant. The days at sea were highly stressful, with the entire crew on constant alert for German wolf packs, and became even more so when the ship's funnel caught fire and the *Axel Johnson* had to drop behind the convoy, leaving it a sitting duck for the U-boats. Fortunately, it was never spotted and managed to limp to port, but it was hardly an atmosphere to inspire the writing of a masterful creative work.

Despite this, Britten composed most of his moody, unorthodox, yet uplifting *A Ceremony of Carols* during his passage home. The piece draws inspiration from many unlikely sources, including poetry from the medieval England of Geoffrey Chaucer (Britten gathered some of this material from a book he purchased when the ship stopped over in Halifax, Nova Scotia).

A Ceremony of Carols was originally composed for a chamber choir and harp. It debuted at London's Wigmore Hall in December 1943, performed by the Morriston Boys' Choir under Britten's direction. It has since been recorded many times by choirs from around the world.

Modern Carols

It all started in 1850 with "Jingle Bells"—the first well-known secular carol. That "one horse open sleigh" opened the door for the twentieth century transformation of Christmas music from reverent and religious themes to fun, sentimental, and sometimes even comical ones.

The Christmas music of today bears little resemblance to the medieval Christian hymns that started the carol tradition. In fact, some modern holiday songs like "Winter Wonderland" and "Frosty the Snowman" don't even mention Christmas at all, but instead celebrate the delights of the winter season. And novelty songs such as "The Night Santa Went Crazy" and "Rudolph the Red-Nosed Reindeer" focus on bringing out the lighter side of the holiday.

With the recording technology of the modern era, the tradition of carolling door-to-door quickly waned as radio and then television began broadcasting our favourite Christmas music right into our homes. And with stars such as Bing Crosby, Gene Autry, and Elvis Presley singing seasonal songs, Christmas music exploded into a big business. Nowadays, it seems like every major recording artist has a Christmas album for sale.

Of course, carol writing didn't die out completely. Some twentieth century composers such as Alfred Burt ("Caroling, Caroling") and Katherine Kennicott Davis ("The Little Drummer Boy") kept the tradition going, but they were the exceptions in the modern era. For the most part, the twentieth century changed the tone of Christmas music forever.

Brainteaser Trivia

(Answers on page 221)

Pumpkin Pies

1. Name the Christmas song that holds the distinction of being the fastest selling single of all time in the United Kingdom.
   a. "White Christmas"
   b. "Last Christmas"
   c. "Blue Christmas"
   d. "Do They Know It's Christmas?"

2. Which holiday song was a hit for Harry Belafonte during the 1957 Christmas season?
   a. "Go Tell It on the Mountain"
   b. "O Little Town of Bethlehem"
   c. "Mary's Boy Child"
   d. "Twelve Days of Christmas"

3. In 1977, Bing Crosby performed the duet "Little Drummer Boy/Peace on Earth" on his holiday special *Bing Crosby's Merrie Olde Christmas* (his last television appearance before his death). Which famous rock star (described by Crosby as "a clean-cut kid") performed with him?

   a. Mick Jagger   c. Frank Zappa
   b. Bruce Springsteen   d. David Bowie

4. Which sibling singing group released the 1970 holiday hit "Merry Christmas Darling"?

   a. The Jackson Five   c. Donny and Marie
   b. The Carpenters   d. The Bee Gees

5. Which charity has received the proceeds (over fifty-five million dollars) of the *A Very Special Christmas* celebrity benefit series of albums?

   a. Ronald McDonald House   c. Make-a-Wish Foundation
   b. UNICEF   d. Special Olympics

6. Which non-holiday song is referenced in the 1957 Christmas standard "Jingle Bell Rock"?

   a. "Twist and Shout"   c. "Jailhouse Rock"
   b. "All Shook Up"   d. "Rock Around the Clock"

7. What Christmas song was inspired by a widely circulated email, which in turn was based on a story in *Chicken Soup for the Christian Soul*?

    a. "The Christmas Box"   c. "Blue Christmas"

    b. "Pretty Paper"   d. "The Christmas Shoes"

8. Which famous composer of "The Christmas Song" was also known by the nickname The Velvet Fog?

    a. Dean Martin   c. Mel Torme

    b. Frank Sinatra   d. Louis Armstrong

9. The nostalgic "I'll Be Home for Christmas" became the most requested song by soldiers and their loved ones during which war?

    a. The First World War   c. The Korean War

    b. The Second World War   d. The Vietnam War

10. What kind of meteorological event inspired the lyrics to "The Christmas Song"?

    a. A blizzard   b. A hurricane   c. A flood   d. A heat wave

11. The proceeds of the 1984 song "Do They Know It's Christmas?" were donated to relief efforts in which African country?

    a. Sudan   b. Rwanda   c. Ethiopia   d. Somalia

12. In Bob and Doug Mackenzie's hit parody of the song "The Twelve Days of Christmas," what do they substitute for the partridge in the pear tree?

a. A pound of back bacon   c. A beer

b. A turtleneck   d. A comic book

13. In what month of the year did songwriters Jule Styne and Sammy Cahn write their holiday hit "Let It Snow"?

a. March   b. July   c. October   d. December

14. Which former member of The Beatles wrote and recorded the 1971 protest song "Happy Christmas (War Is Over)"?

a. George Harrison   c. Paul McCartney

b. John Lennon   d. Ringo Starr

15. In the 1949 song "C-H-R-I-S-T-M-A-S," each letter of the song's title stands for something meaningful about the holiday. According to the lyrics, what does the last "S" stand for?

a. Snow   b. Santa Claus   c. Sleigh   d. Shepherds

16. During the Vietnam War, a Christmas song was selected for use by the United States military as a radio signal for the immediate evacuation of Saigon. Which song was it?

a. "White Christmas"   c. "O Come All Ye Faithful"

b. "Silent Night"   d. "Jingle Bells"

17. Which character in the lyrics of the well-known Christmas song "Do You Hear What I Hear?" asks the title question?

    a. The night wind　　　　c. The shepherd boy
    b. The little lamb　　　　d. The mighty king

18. Which British pop band released the hit holiday single "Last Christmas" in 1984?

    a. Bananarama　　　　c. Wham!
    b. Culture Club　　　　d. Duran Duran

19. Which American girl-group released a holiday album entitled "8 Days of Christmas" in 2001?

    a. Destiny's Child　　　　c. Wilson Phillips
    b. The Spice Girls　　　　d. TLC

20. In 1967, which famous musical group released the holiday song "Christmas Time (Is Here Again)" exclusively to members of their fan club (holding back releasing it as a single until 1995)?

    a. The Rolling Stones　　　　c. The Guess Who
    b. The Beatles　　　　d. Pink Floyd

21. In the protest song "Happy Christmas (War Is Over)," which war is the song title referring to?
    a. The Gulf War
    b. The Korean War
    c. The Vietnam War
    d. The Cold War

22. Name the only Christmas song ever to hold the number one spot on the American music charts on Christmas Day.
    a. "White Christmas"
    b. "Blue Christmas"
    c. "Silver Bells"
    d. "The Chipmunk Song"

23. What was the original title of the popular Christmas song "Little Drummer Boy"?
    a. "Carol of the Drum"
    b. "Pa-Rum-Pum-Pum-Pum"
    c. "Gift for the King"
    d. "Song for a Saviour"

24. What Elvis Presley holiday song was written by his bodyguard?
    a. "Blue Christmas"
    b. "If Every Day Was Like Christmas"
    c. "Santa Bring My Baby Back (To Me)"
    d. "If I Get Home on Christmas Day"

Plum Puddings

25. Which twentieth century screen siren released a holiday album entitled "Wild Christmas" in 1966?

    a. Madonna
    b. Marilyn Monroe
    c. Mae West
    d. Raquel Welch

26. In what unusual location was Richard Smith when he wrote the lyrics to the holiday favourite "Winter Wonderland" in 1934?

    a. An amusement park
    b. A tuberculosis sanatorium
    c. A public restroom
    d. A grocery store checkout line

27. Who sang "Christmas in Hollis" on the original release of *A Very Special Christmas* back in 1987?

    a. Céline Dion
    b. Paul McCartney
    c. Run-D.M.C.
    d. Jon Bon Jovi

28. Which famous country music singer wrote and gave the Christmas song "Pretty Paper" to Roy Orbison, who made it a hit in 1964?

    a. Johnny Cash
    b. Loretta Lynn
    c. Patsy Cline
    d. Willie Nelson

29. According to Mel Torme, how long did it take him and co-writer Bob Welles to write "The Christmas Song (Chestnuts Roasting On an Open Fire)" back in 1946?

a. Forty-five minutes

b. Four and a half hours

c. Forty-five days

d. Twelve months

30. Which of the following Christmas hits did *not* appear on the American pop charts in 1949?

a. "Rudolph the Red-Nosed Reindeer"

b. "Here Comes Santa Claus"

c. "Blue Christmas"

d. "Frosty the Snowman"

31. What Christian vocal group first recorded the song "The Christmas Shoes," written by two of its members?

a. NewSong

b. The Interior Castle

c. Go Fish

d. Adonai

32. American Jewish songwriters have composed many of the most beloved modern Christmas songs. Which of the following holiday standards was *not* written by a Jewish songwriter?

a. "White Christmas"

b. "The Christmas Song"

c. "Silver Bells"

d. "Do You Hear What I Hear?"

33. Upon its release in the 1950s, which popular Christmas song was banned in several states because its lyrics were deemed too scandalous?

    a. "Blue Christmas"
    b. "Rudolph the Red-Nosed Reindeer"
    c. "Jingle Bell Rock
    d. "I Saw Mommy Kissing Santa Claus"

34. How old was Mel Torme when he wrote the music to "The Christmas Song"?

    a. Nineteen   b. Twenty-nine   c. Thirty-nine   d. Forty-nine

35. Which female pop superstar wrote and recorded the 1994 single "All I Want for Christmas Is You"?

    a. Céline Dion   c. Madonna
    b. Whitney Houston   d. Mariah Carey

36. Name the singer who released "Jingle Bell Rock" back in 1957.

    a. Elvis Presley   c. Bill Haley
    b. Bobby Helms   d. Cliff Richard

37. Which former Beatle released "Wonderful Christmas Time" in 1982?

    a. Paul McCartney   c. George Harrison
    b. John Lennon   d. Ringo Starr

38. Which famous soul singer of the 1960s put together the eclectic yuletide compilation entitled *Funky Christmas*?

a. James Brown

b. Aretha Franklin

c. Marvin Gaye

d. Wilson Pickett

39. How old was Little Miss Dynamite, Brenda Lee, when she recorded "Rockin' Around the Christmas Tree" back in 1958?

a. Thirteen   b. Fifteen   c. Seventeen   d. Nineteen

40. Why was Bing Crosby forced to re-record his best-selling song "White Christmas" in 1947—five years after the original one was released?

a. The original master disc had worn out

b. New lyrics were added

c. A change was made to the tune

d. It wasn't selling anymore

41. Which rock 'n' roll band re-released the mournful R&B holiday song "Please Come Home for Christmas" in 1978?

a. Styx   b. Foreigner   c. The Eagles   d. Journey

42. Which of the following is the unlikely title of a Christmas song by recording artist Chris de Burgh?
    a. "Lady in Red"
    b. "A Spaceman Came Travelling"
    c. "Spanish Train"
    d. "Don't Pay the Ferryman"

43. Despite the misleading name, which of the following Joni Mitchell songs has a Christmastime theme?
    a. "Big Yellow Taxi"   c. "River"
    b. "Snakes and Ladders"   d. "Chelsea Morning"

44. "Mele Kalikimaka" ("The Hawaiian Christmas Song") was recorded in 1950 by which famous singer?
    a. Frank Sinatra   c. Nat King Cole
    b. Perry Como   d. Bing Crosby

45. "Santa Baby" is a holiday song about a hugely extravagant Christmas list. Which of the following women did *not* record a version of it?
    a. Eartha Kitt   c. Marilyn Monroe
    b. Kylie Minogue   d. Madonna

46. Which famous crooner popularized the song "There's No Place Like Home for the Holidays"?
    a. Bing Crosby
    b. Perry Como
    c. Nat King Cole
    d. Tony Bennett

47. Name the only former Beatle ever to release a Christmas album (1999's *I Wanna Be Santa Claus*).
    a. George Harrison
    b. John Lennon
    c. Paul McCartney
    d. Ringo Starr

48. Which former Beatle released the 1974 holiday single "Ding Dong, Ding Dong"?
    a. George Harrison
    b. John Lennon
    c. Paul McCartney
    d. Ringo Starr

49. When Leroy Anderson and the Boston Pops Orchestra introduced the hugely popular instrumental piece "Sleigh Ride," they featured a variety of realistic sound effects. Which of the following was *not* one of those effects?
    a. Sleigh bells
    b. Whip cracks
    c. Clopping hooves
    d. Giddy-ups

50. Who wrote and recorded the holiday parody "The Night Santa Went Crazy"?

a. Steve Martin

b. Spinal Tap

c. Weird Al Yankovic

d. Eddie Murphy

Chestnuts

51. Along with "Rudolph the Red-Nosed Reindeer," "Silver and Gold," and "Rockin' Around the Christmas Tree," which other famous holiday standard was penned by songwriter Johnny Marks?

a. "I Saw Mommy Kissing Santa Claus"

b. "Holly Jolly Christmas"

c. "Santa Claus Is Coming to Town"

d. "Jingle Bell Rock"

52. Which legendary rock 'n' roller was the first to record "Run Rudolph Run" in 1958?

a. Elvis Presley

b. Little Richard

c. Buddy Holly

d. Chuck Berry

53. Which popular American country music star recorded the song "Santa Looked a Lot Like Daddy" in 1992?

a. Willie Nelson

b. Kenny Rogers

c. Clint Black

d. Garth Brooks

54. Band Aid has made several different celebrity recordings of the African relief song "Do They Know It's Christmas?" In which of the following years was a version of this song *not* released?

a. 1984   b. 1989   c. 1993   d. 2004

55. Leroy Anderson, the composer of the 1948 Christmas song "Sleigh Ride," was also the composer and arranger for which well-known orchestra (which introduced the piece)?

a. Boston Pops
b. Glenn Miller Orchestra
c. London Symphony Orchestra
d. New York Philharmonic

56. Which famous duo released the song "Christmas Eve Can Kill You" in 1972?

a. The Everly Brothers   c. Captain & Tennille
b. Sonny and Cher   d. Donny and Marie

57. Which holiday song appeared on the flip side of Brenda Lee's gold-selling hit "Rockin' Around the Christmas Tree"?

a. "Papa Noël"   c. "Daddy Claus"
b. "Father Christmas"   d. "Grandfather Frost"

58. Alfred Burt was a young musician who composed fifteen Christmas carols between 1942 and 1954. Name the last carol Burt composed, which was finished one day before his untimely death at the age of thirty-three.

   a. "The Star Carol"
   b. "Caroling, Caroling"
   c. "Some Children See Him"
   d. "All on a Christmas Morning"

59. In 1911, songwriters Charles N. Daniels and Earle C. Jones composed the sentimental holiday tune "I Think of Home and _____ When It's Christmas Time." Fill in the blank.

   a. Mother   b. Baby   c. Jesus   d. Puppies

60. Name the 1996 tongue-in-cheek Christmas album released by the American punk rock group, The Vandals.

   a. *Oi To the World!*   c. *Uncle Santa*
   b. *Christmas Kung-Fu*   d. *O Holy Sock*

61. Which rock duo released a Christmas song entitled "Candy Cane Children" in 2002?

   a. Steely Dan   c. Hall and Oates
   b. The White Stripes   d. Evanescence

62. Name the wildly popular Irish Christmas song that opens with lyrics about Christmas Eve in a drunk tank.

    a. "Fairytale of New York"   c. "Come Fill Up Your Glasses"

    b. "Christmas in Killarney"   d. "The Wexford Carol"

63. Which American jazz legend recorded the song "Santa Claus Got Stuck in My Chimney" back in 1950?

    a. Duke Ellington   c. Ella Fitzgerald

    b. Louis Armstrong   d. Billie Holiday

64. Which British progressive rock band released a 2003 Christmas album featuring songs such as "Ring Out Solstice Bells," "We Five Kings," and "Jack Frost and the Hooded Crow"?

    a. Pink Floyd   b. Jethro Tull   c. Yes   d. Genesis

65. The B-side of which famous holiday hit featured the song "Captain Santa Claus (and his Reindeer Space Patrol)"?

    a. "Blue Christmas"

    b. "Do They Know It's Christmas?"

    c. "Jingle Bell Rock"

    d. "Rudolph the Red-Nosed Reindeer"

66. Recorded by the Trans-Siberian Orchestra in 1996, "Christmas Eve/Sarajevo 12/24" is a medley of two Christmas carols: "God Rest Ye Merry, Gentlemen" and a heavy metal version of which other one?

    a. "Carol of the Bells"
    b. "Silent Night"
    c. "We Wish You a Merry Christmas"
    d. "It Came Upon a Midnight Clear"

67. Which rock star refers to Santa Claus as a "bearded weirdy" in the 1973 holiday single "Ho Ho Ho (Who'd Be a Turkey at Christmas)"?

    a. Elton John   c. Robert Plant
    b. Mick Jagger   d. John Lennon

68. The son of which great modern tenor composed the Christmas song "Un Nuevo Siglo"?

    a. Luciano Pavarotti   c. José Carreras
    b. Placido Domingo   d. Mario Lanza

69. The idea for what Christmas song was first written on a Piggly Wiggly shopping bag?

    a. "Blue Christmas"   c. "Caroling, Caroling"
    b. "Pretty Paper"   d. "Thank God for Kids"

70. What poem, written by lovesick teenager Frank Pooler in 1946, became a big hit after Richard Carpenter set it to music two decades later?

    a. "Caroling, Caroling"   c. "Do You Hear What I Hear?"
    b. "Merry Christmas, Darling" d. "Home for the Holidays"

71. Who first recorded "Blue Christmas"?

    a. Elvis Presley   c. Hugo Winterhalter
    b. Leroy Anderson   d. Herb Alpert

72. Songwriter Mitchell Parish added lyrics to Leroy Anderson's "Sleigh Ride" two years after it was composed. Name another hit song that Parish wrote.

    a. "Stars Fell on Alabama"   c. "Maryland, My Maryland"
    b. "Georgia on My Mind"   d. "California, Here I Come"

73. Carl Sigman, who wrote the words for the winter favourite "A Marshmallow World," also penned the lyrics for this Christmas song.

    a. "Home for the Holidays"
    b. "I'll Be Home for Christmas"
    c. "There's No Christmas Like a Home Christmas"
    d. "Up on the Housetop"

Did You Know?

"Do They Know It's Christmas?"

This song was written in late 1984 after a BBC report by Michael Buerk was aired on television, exposing the famine in Ethiopia to the eyes of the world. Bob Geldof of the Irish rock group The Boomtown Rats was immediately inspired by the broadcast and, together with Midge Ure, wrote the song in hope of raising money and awareness for the devastated population of Ethiopia.

In a matter of weeks, Band Aid was formed—a supergroup of British and Irish musicians, all of whom donated their time and talent to record the song for the cause. Among others, the band included Phil Collins, Bono (of U2), George Michael, Bananarama, Sting, and Boy George.

The recording studio donated its services as well, and on November 25, 1984, between eleven A.M. and seven P.M., the recording session took place (and was filmed for the song's video).

The result became an overnight sensation. According to Geldof's website: "The record was released on 15 December and went straight to number 1 in the UK pop charts outselling all the other records in the chart put together. It became the fastest selling single of all time in the UK, selling a million in the first week alone. It stayed at Number 1 for five weeks, selling over 3 million copies...."

With the promise that every penny earned from the song would go to relief efforts in Ethiopia, the single quickly raised millions of dollars. After public pressure (spearheaded by Geldof), the British government—led at the time by Margaret Thatcher—reluctantly donated the tax money collected on the single to the cause as well.

Band Aid's success with "Do They Know It's Christmas?" inspired other charity recordings and concerts around the world, including Live Aid, Farm Aid, USA for Africa, Northern Lights (Canada), and Band fur Afrika (Germany).

The Alfred Burt Carols

Alfred Burt was one of the last modern composers of traditional, religious-themed Christmas carols. Known collectively as "The Alfred Burt Carols," he wrote fifteen in total on a creative spree between 1942 and 1954.

He came by his talent for music naturally. Born in 1920, Burt was just a baby when his father, a self-taught musician, started a tradition of writing an annual carol to be sent out as their family Christmas card.

By the time he was ten years old, Burt was teaching himself how to play the cornet. Music soon became the driving force in his life. He earned a degree from the University of Michigan School of Music in 1942. That same year, he took over his father's tradition and composed his first carol for the Burt family Christmas card—"Christmas Cometh

Caroling." He churned out a new Christmas card carol every year for the next twelve years, composing the music while his father and family friend Wihla Hutson wrote the lyrics.

Many of them have gone on to become quite well known. Burt's list of carols includes "All on a Christmas Morning," "Some Children See Him," "O, Hearken Ye," and perhaps the most famous, "Caroling, Caroling."

As the list of carols grew, so did interest in Burt's music. By 1950, the family Christmas card list had gone from fifty names to over four hundred fifty.

But in 1953, everything changed when Burt was diagnosed with lung cancer. At the young age of thirty-three he was given less than a year to live. With time and Christmases running out, Burt worked hard in his final months to compose four more carols—enough to accomplish his dream of recording an album.

His last composition, "The Star Carol," was completed on February 5, 1954. Alfred Burt died the next day, only one hour before his recording contract was delivered by courier from Columbia Records.

"The Christmas Shoes"

If the story weren't so well documented, you'd think it was the stuff of urban myth. The origin of the hit song "The Christmas Shoes" is at once strange, sad, and inspiring.

The story begins in the 1970s in Kansas, where a woman named Helga Schmidt was doing some last-minute Christmas shopping at a local discount store. As she recounted later in a story she titled "Golden Shoes for Jesus," she was delayed at the checkout counter by two small children, a boy and a girl, who were trying to buy a cheap pair of gold-coloured slippers for their mother. They put all the money they had on the counter but were about three dollars short. When the clerk explained that it wasn't enough, the little girl started to cry. Moved by a child's distress so close to Christmas, Schmidt paid the difference. When she asked the children why they wanted the slippers so badly, she was told that their mother was dying and they wanted to give her shoes that were the same colour as the streets of heaven.

"Silently I thanked God for using these children to remind me of the true spirit of giving," Schmidt wrote later.

Schmidt submitted the story to her church newspaper. From there, it was picked up and republished in other church publications until it eventually ended up in the hands of the editors of the hugely successful *Chicken Soup* books, who included it in *Chicken Soup for the Christian Soul,* published in 1997. By then, the author's name had been lost.

The story touched many people's hearts and it soon began to be circulated by email on the internet, where it was read by millions. One of them was Eddie Carswell of the pop Christian singing group NewSong. He and another member of the group at the time, Leonard Ahlstrom, turned Schmidt's story into a hit Christmas song in 2000. One year later, a book based on the events was written by Donna VanLiere and has since become a perennial holiday-season best-seller. The book in turn spawned a made-for-television movie starring Rob Lowe, which was first aired by CBS in 2002 and is now repeated annually.

You'd think that, after having created a Christmas industry based on her personal experience, Helga Schmidt would be a wealthy woman. Alas, that is not the case. She says she has never received one cent in royalties, and didn't even get a credit in the TV movie. But, ever philosophical, she was quoted in *The Mennonite Weekly Review* a few years ago as saying: "Other people can get rich, but I'm rich in spirit because of it."

There is a dark side to this inspiring tale, however. Apparently, some unscrupulous scam artists are now using little children to bilk generous people into buying articles of clothing for their sick moms at Christmastime and then returning them for cash the next day. So, if you see a sobbing waif at the local Wal-Mart this Christmas season, be wary.

Carols on Stage,
Screen, Radio,
and TV

Many of today's most popular Christmas songs were originally introduced to the world by way of movies, television, theatre, radio, or other popular media. The holiday classic "White Christmas" was first heard on the radio, "Silver Bells" and "Have Yourself a Merry Little Christmas" debuted on film, while others such as "Holly Jolly Christmas" and "All I Want for Christmas Is My Two Front Teeth" first came to the world through our TV sets.

Some of those performances have become holiday season standards over the years. Who can forget the haunting, melancholy rendition of "Have Yourself a Merry Little Christmas" by Judy Garland in the film *Meet Me in St. Louis* or the gleefully diabolical "You're a Mean One, Mr. Grinch" from the TV special *How the Grinch Stole Christmas!*?

Most of the songs we write about in this section come from the twentieth century, but some, like "The Coventry Carol," debuted on the stage all the way back in the Renaissance era.

Whether introducing new carols or re-playing old standards, entertainers from the stage, screen, radio, and TV have played a vital role in bringing us our Christmas music over the years. This chapter recalls the memories of those performances and performers.

Brainteaser Trivia

(Answers on page 223)

Pumpkin Pies

1. In the Broadway musical *Mame,* the title character and her nephew sing the song "We Need a Little Christmas" to lift their spirits during which dark twentieth century period?

   a. The First World War   c. The Second World War

   b. The Great Depression   d. The Vietnam War

2. Which popular television special introduced the world to the Johnny Marks hit, "A Holly Jolly Christmas"?

   a. *How the Grinch Stole Christmas!*

   b. *Frosty the Snowman*

   c. *Rudolph the Red-Nosed Reindeer*

   d. *A Charlie Brown Christmas*

3. "Have Yourself a Merry Little Christmas" was first introduced in which Judy Garland movie?

   a. *The Wizard of Oz*   c. *A Star Is Born*

   b. *Meet Me in St. Louis*   d. *Easter Parade*

4. Which famous fashion model debuted the Christmas song "Mistletoe and Wine" in the 1986 British TV musical *The Little Match Girl*?

   a. Cindy Crawford   c. Twiggy

   b. Iman   d. Tyra Banks

5. According to the lyrics of "You're a Mean One, Mr. Grinch" (from the 1966 animated television special *How the Grinch Stole Christmas!*), what are the three words that best describe the title character?

   a. Skink. Skank. Skunk.   c. Stink. Stank. Stunk.

   b. Slink. Slank. Slunk.   d. Old. Fat. Mean.

6. What popular comedian, never considered much of a singer, introduced "Silver Bells" in one of his movies?

   a. Jack Benny   c. Bob Hope

   b. George Burns   d. Eddie Cantor

7. Name the jazz pianist who wrote the music for the hugely popular television special, *A Charlie Brown Christmas*.

   a. Vince Guaraldi   c. Dave Brubeck

   b. Bill Evans   d. Keith Jarrett

8. Which snowless U.S. city is mentioned in the opening lines of "White Christmas"?

   a. Los Angeles b. Miami   c. Dallas   d. San Diego

9. What song from the Rodgers and Hammerstein musical *The Sound of Music* has been adopted as a Christmas song?

   a. "Maria"   c. "My Favorite Things"
   b. "Edelweiss"   d. "Climb Ev'ry Mountain"

10. Which Academy Award winning actor sang "A Holly Jolly Christmas" in the 1964 animated television special *Rudolph the Red-Nosed Reindeer*?

    a. Burl Ives   c. Gene Kelly
    b. Clint Eastwood   d. Marlon Brando

11. Which traditional carol is *loo-loo*'d by the Peanuts gang in the final scene of the television special *A Charlie Brown Christmas*?

    a. "Deck the Halls"   c. "Good King Wenceslas"
    b. "Away in a Manger"   d. "Hark! The Herald Angels Sing"

12. Which singing TV family released a Christmas album featuring the original song "My Christmas Card to You" in 1971?

    a. The Brady Bunch   c. The Partridge Family
    b. The Osmond Family   d. The Von Trapp Family

13. Which television cartoon characters released the 1993 holiday album *Crock O' Christmas,* featuring songs such as "We Wish You a Hairy Chestwig" and "The Twelve Days of Yaksmas"?

a. The Simpsons

b. Tom and Jerry

c. Ren and Stimpy

d. Rocky and Bullwinkle

14. Which famous British actor played the role of Jacob Marley's Ghost in *Scrooge,* the 1970 musical adaptation of *A Christmas Carol*?

a. Sir Alec Guinness

b. Sir Laurence Olivier

c. Sir Anthony Hopkins

d. Hugh Grant

15. Which 2000 holiday song inspired a CBS made-for-TV movie of the same name starring Rob Lowe and Kimberly Williams?

a. "The Christmas Shoes"

b. "Star of Bethlehem"

c. "A Heart to Hold You"

d. "I'm Your Angel"

16. Which hit television comedy released a Christmas album in 2000 featuring holiday songs by the singer Vonda Shepard?

a. *The Simpsons*

b. *Seinfeld*

c. *Friends*

d. *Ally McBeal*

17. In "We Need a Little Christmas," from *Mame,* what musical instrument is said to accompany the carols?

    a. Piano   c. Spinet

    b. Violin   d. Accordion

18. Meredith Willson, the composer of the 1951 Broadway song "It's Beginning To Look A Lot Like Christmas" went on to write which 1957 smash hit musical?

    a. *Hello Dolly*   c. *West Side Story*

    b. *Oklahoma!*   d. *The Music Man*

19. In addition to "White Christmas," which other popular Christmas song was featured in the movie *Holiday Inn*?

    a. "I'll Be Home for Christmas"

    b. "Winter Wonderland"

    c. "Jingle Bell Rock"

    d. "Happy Holidays"

20. What Tony Award winning Broadway musical based on the opera *La bohème* opens on Christmas Eve in a Greenwich Village loft?

    a. *Hair*   b. *Oliver!*   c. *Rent*   d. *Mame*

Plum Puddings

21. Thurl Ravenscroft, the singer of "You're a Mean One, Mr. Grinch," (from the 1966 animated television special *How the Grinch Stole Christmas!*), was also the voice of which famous cartoon character?

    a. Bugs Bunny

    b. Tony the Tiger

    c. Fred Flintstone

    d. Mickey Mouse

22. On which popular variety show did Alvin and the Chipmunks appear lip-synching "The Chipmunk Song"?

    a. *The Tonight Show*

    b. *The Smothers Brothers*

    c. *The Perry Como Show*

    d. *The Ed Sullivan Show*

23. Which Annie Lennox and Al Green duet was featured on the soundtrack to the 1988 Christmas movie *Scrooged*?

    a. "Sweet Dreams"

    b. "Why?"

    c. "Walking on Broken Glass"

    d. "Put a Little Love in Your Heart"

24. Which well-known crooner sang "Silent Night" in the 1944 film *Going My Way*?

    a. Bing Crosby

    b. Dean Martin

    c. Mel Torme

    d. Perry Como

25. "It's Beginning to Look a Lot Like Christmas" was included in the 1963 Broadway show *Here's Love,* a musical based on which famous Christmas movie?

a. *It's a Wonderful Life*

b. *Miracle on 34th Street*

c. *The Bishop's Wife*

d. *Holiday Inn*

26. "Kidnap the Sandy Claws" appears on the soundtrack of which 1993 holiday movie?

a. *The Santa Clause*

b. *The Nightmare Before Christmas*

c. *National Lampoon's Christmas Vacation*

d. *Ernest Saves Christmas*

27. Which British singer performed the opening lines to "Do They Know It's Christmas?" in the famous 1984 recording session video?

a. George Michael

b. David Bowie

c. Simon LeBon

d. Paul Young

28. In which 1951 movie did the hugely popular Christmas song "Silver Bells" receive its screen debut?

a. *A Christmas Carol*

b. *Father's Little Dividend*

c. *The Lemon Drop Kid*

d. *The Day the Earth Stood Still*

29. Which famous singer/actor/comedian sang the title song in the 1969 animated television special *Frosty the Snowman*?

a. Jerry Lewis

b. Jamie Foxx

c. Bob Hope

d. Jimmy Durante

30. Which famous country music star sang "Where Are You Christmas?" on the soundtrack to the 2000 hit movie *How the Grinch Stole Christmas!*?

a. Carrie Underwood

b. Martina McBride

c. Reba McEntire

d. Faith Hill

31. Which of the many different film versions of *A Christmas Carol* featured the song "Oh, What a Merry Christmas Day"?

a. *Mickey's Christmas Carol*

b. *The Muppet Christmas Carol*

c. *A Flintstone Christmas Carol*

d. *Scrooge*

32. The songs "Somewhere in My Memory" and "Star of Bethlehem" were composed for which 1990 blockbuster holiday movie?

a. *The Santa Clause*

b. *Scrooged*

c. *Home Alone*

d. *All I Want for Christmas*

33. How did the second line originally read in an early draft of "Have Yourself a Merry Little Christmas"?

    a. "Let your heart be bright"   c. "And a silent night"

    b. "May the day be white"   d. "It may be your last"

34. Which American pop singer performed the song "Believe" on the soundtrack to the 2004 holiday movie *The Polar Express*?

    a. Justin Timberlake   c. Josh Groban

    b. Ricky Martin   d. Clay Aiken

35. How old was screen siren Mae West when she released the holiday songs "Santa Come Up and See Me" and "Put the Loot in the Boot, Santa"?

    a. Twenty-three   c. Forty-three

    b. Thirty-three   d. Seventy-three

36. The first movie to tell the story of how the carol "Silent Night" came to be written was filmed in 1933. In what language was it?

    a. German   b. French   c. English   d. Polish

37. Which holiday song is the crowd at George Bailey's house singing in the final moments of *It's a Wonderful Life*?

    a. "Joy to the World"   c. "Silent Night"

    b. "Auld Lang Syne"   d. "Deck the Halls"

38. Who had to be persuaded by his wife to introduce "Santa Claus Is Coming to Town" on his radio show?

a. Eddie Cantor

b. George Burns

c. Fred Allen

d. Jack Benny

39. "All I Want for Christmas Is My Two Front Teeth" was first introduced in the 1940s on which famous singer's radio show?

a. Frank Sinatra

b. Sammy Davis, Jr.

c. Perry Como

d. Dean Martin

40. "Have Yourself a Merry Little Christmas" was introduced in the movie *Meet Me in St. Louis,* which was set in the time of the World's Fair in that city. What year was it?

a. 1898   b. 1903   c. 1917   d. 1939

Chestnuts

41. The 1955 song "Nuttin' for Christmas" was first introduced on what legendary television show?

a. *The Ed Sullivan Show*

b. *The Burns and Allen Show*

c. *The Milton Berle Show*

d. *The Adventures of Ozzie and Harriet*

42. Which rousing carol was sung during the closing scene of the only Christmas-themed episode of *The Andy Griffith Show*?

   a. "Joy to the World"   c. "Hark! the Herald Angels Sing"
   b. "Deck the Halls"   d. "O Christmas Tree"

43. Which Band Aid celebrity singer had to be woken up and flown in by Concorde to make it on time for the recording session and video filming of 1984's holiday hit "Do They Know It's Christmas?"?

   a. Bono   c. Bob Geldof
   b. Boy George   d. Phil Collins

44. "The Coventry Carol" was introduced in a sixteenth century pageant put on by the Shearmen and Tailors Guild of Coventry. The script called for the carol to be sung by the women of Bethlehem for what purpose?

   a. To praise the Lord
   b. To announce the birth of Jesus
   c. To quiet their babies
   d. To entertain the audience during intermission

45. Ray Evans and Jay Livingston, the composers of "Silver Bells," originally considered calling the song by another name until Livingston's wife stepped in and changed their minds. What was the proposed name?

a. "Tinkle Bell"   c. "Ding-a-Ling Bell"
b. "Winkle Bell"   d. "Sprinkle Bell"

46. In the late 1950s, which Christmas album earned three Grammy Awards and a nomination for Record of the Year?

a. *A Charlie Brown Christmas*
b. *The Chipmunk Song ("Christmas Don't Be Late")*
c. *The Beach Boys' Christmas Album*
d. *Rockin' Around the Christmas Tree*

47. In what stage show was "We Need a Little Christmas" introduced?

a. *Pal Joey*   b. *Mame*   c. *Oklahoma!*   d. *Oliver!*

48. In what year did the show debut?

a. 1960   b. 1966   c. 1970   d. 1976

49. The song "Toyland" debuted in the 1903 operetta *Babes in Toyland*. What distinguishes this song from most other holiday favourites?

a. It's written about children   c. It makes no mention of Christmas
b. It's sung in the key of F   d. Its lyrics don't rhyme

50. Judy Garland requested a re-write of the song "Have Yourself a Merry Little Christmas" before agreeing to sing it in the 1944 movie *Meet Me in St. Louis*. What was her problem with the original lyrics?

a. They were too hard to pronounce

b. They were too controversial

c. They were too sombre

d. They didn't mention Christmas

51. *Amahl and the Night Visitors* is a Christmas opera that holds the distinction of being the first opera ever written specifically for television. It was inspired by *The Adoration of the Magi*, painted by which famous Dutch artist?

a. Hieronymus Bosch

b. Vincent van Gogh

c. Rembrandt van Rijn

d. Jan Vermeer

52. Irving Berlin, the composer of *Holiday Inn*'s "White Christmas," changed his name soon after becoming a songwriter. Which name was he born with in 1888?

a. Israel Baline

b. Ian Battenberg

c. Igor Bronsky

d. Ingmar Bornstein

53. Besides "It's Beginning to Look a Lot Like Christmas," name another Christmas song from the Meredith Willson musical *Here's Love*.

a. "Pine Cones and Holly Berries"
b. "Greenwillow Christmas"
c. "I Can't Remember Christmas"
d. "Hard Candy Christmas"

54. In the only holiday episode of *The Brady Bunch,* which carol does Mrs. Brady sing in church after having her voice miraculously restored to her on Christmas?

a. "Silent Night"   c. "Joy to the World"
b. "O Come All Ye Faithful"   d. "The Boar's Head Carol"

55. What carol played in the background during the final scene of the last episode of season five of *The Sopranos* television series in 2006?

a. "The First Nowell"   c. "O Little Town of Bethlehem"
b. "Silent Night"   d. "Away in a Manger"

56. Which of the following was voted Best Christmas Song of All Time in three consecutive years (2004, 2005, 2006) by polls on the British music TV channel VH1 UK?

a. "Hark! The Herald Angels Sing"
b. "Do They Know It's Christmas?"
c. "White Christmas"
d. "Fairytale of New York"

57. Which U.S. president changed the dinner hour at the White House so he and his family could watch Judy Garland's Christmas special on television?

a. Dwight D. Eisenhower   c. Lyndon Johnson
b. John F. Kennedy   d. Richard Nixon

58. The song "Turkey Lurkey Time" comes from what Broadway show?

a. *Promises, Promises*   c. *Pal Joey*
b. *Company*   d. *The Fantasticks*

59. In "Turkey Lurkey Time," which of these words is *not* used to describe Christmas?

a. Icy   b. Snowy   c. Mistletoey   d. Blowy

60. What comedic actor wrote the lyrics and performed the "Santa Song" on the *Saturday Night Live* show of December 11, 1993?

a. Mel Brooks

b. Adam Sandler

c. Chevy Chase

d. Tim Allen

61. What London stage musical composed by Sir Elton John contains the song "Merry Christmas Maggie Thatcher"?

a. *Greenwillow*

b. *Billy Elliot*

c. *Subways Are for Sleeping*

d. *Stop the World, I Want to Get Off*

62. The tune for "The Parade of the Wooden Soldiers" from the operetta *Babes in Toyland* originated in what country?

a. France   b. Austria   c. Germany   d. Belgium

Did You Know?

Musical History

With a songbook that includes "No Business Like Show Business," "God Bless America," "Blue Skies," and "Easter Parade" to his credit, Irving Berlin is inarguably the quintessential American songwriter. But nothing he wrote has ever compared in scale to the smashing success of his 1940 hit "White Christmas."

Sung by Bing Crosby and Marjorie Reynolds in the 1942 movie *Holiday Inn,* it won Berlin an Academy Award for Best Song (1943) and earned him a place in the history books as the composer of the most popular song of all time.

Over the years, "White Christmas" has become an industry all to itself. Reportedly recorded in just eighteen minutes in its original version, it has sold over one hundred twenty-five million copies; been translated into languages from Japanese to Yiddish; been covered by a range of performers that includes Barbra Streisand, Bob Marley, Billy Idol, Destiny's Child, and Kiss; played a strategic role in the Vietnam War; and even inspired a book, *White Christmas: The Story of an American Song,* by Jody Rosen (2002, Simon & Schuster Inc.).

In her book, Rosen writes that "White Christmas" became such a huge success because it "resonated with some of the deepest strains in

American culture: yearning for an idealized New England past, belief in the ecumenical magic of the 'merry and bright' Christmas season, pining for the sanctuaries of home and hearth."

Whether it does this for you (or merely sends you running from your radio) it is impossible to deny the fact that this song changed musical history and in doing so has become a permanent fixture of the holiday season.

Tinkle Bell?

Over the years, the 1950 holiday song "Silver Bells" has become a Christmas classic, selling millions of records and appearing regularly on The American Society of Composers, Authors and Publishers annual list of top twenty-five holiday songs.

But would it have been as popular if it had been called something else? On December 25, 2005, Ray Evans spoke to National Public Radio about how he and writing partner Jay Livingston wrote the song and how it almost ended up with a very different name.

In the interview, he explains how the two were songwriters under contract with Paramount studios, but since they hadn't had a hit in a while they were getting nervous about the future of their jobs.

And then along came a film called *The Lemon Drop Kid,* which needed a Christmas song. According to Evans, he and Livingston "had no enthusiasm for writing a Christmas song because we thought, stupidly thank God, that the world had too many Christmas songs already."

As they struggled to come up with a song, they noticed a little bell sitting on one of their desks and knew right away that would be their theme for Christmas.

"And the bell makes a tinkly sound when it's ringing," Evans recalled, "so we'll call our song 'Tinkle Bell.'"

Fortunately for them, Livingston's wife quickly vetoed the name. According to Evans, she was astonished: "'Tinkle Bell'? Are you out of your mind? You can't write a Christmas song with the word 'tinkle' in it. Don't you know what the word 'tinkle' means?"

To which her husband reportedly replied, "I never thought of that!"

Evans and Livingston went back to the drawing board and changed the name of their song to "Silver Bells." And the rest, as they say, is song-writing history!

A Charlie Brown Christmas

The network executives were certain it would be a flop. They thought the pace was too slow, grumbled about the lack of laugh track, and were nervous about how audiences would receive Linus's lisping Bible speech. But as Charles Schulz used to say: "There will always be a market for innocence."

And indeed, he was right. It was a hit—a huge hit. When *A*

Charlie Brown Christmas first aired on December 9, 1965, it grabbed fifty percent of the American viewing audience. Critics and viewers alike loved it.

There had never been anything like it before … or probably since. It was the first prime-time cartoon where children provided all the voices. In fact, most of the children had no acting experience at all and some, too young to read, needed their scripts fed to them line by line.

But complementing the childish voices and simplistic cartoons were the sophisticated jazz sounds of Vince Guaraldi. It was a natural combination. As Guaraldi's website explains, his music "… perfectly balanced Charlie Brown's kid-sized universe."

Guaraldi's sparkling soundtrack became an instant classic. Songs such as "Skating," "Christmas Time is Here," and "My Little Drum" will forever conjure up images of the gang's Christmas play rehearsal, Snoopy's commercialized doghouse, and Charlie Brown's wilting tree. Receiving its television debut in *A Charlie Brown Christmas*, "Linus and Lucy" went on to become the Peanuts unofficial theme song as well as one of the world's most popular jazz standards.

And now, over forty years later, the world can't get enough. *A Charlie Brown Christmas* still runs every December and Guaraldi's soundtrack, which has never been out of print, has become one of the most popular holiday albums of all time.

Children's
Christmas Songs

Since the evolution of Santa Claus and the modernization of toy manufacturing in the nineteenth century, Christmas has increasingly become a child-centred holiday. Much of the season's popular music reflects this trend.

"Up on the Housetop" (written in the mid-nineteenth century) may have been the first Christmas song composed expressly for little children. Other songs such as "Jolly Old St. Nicholas" and "Toyland" soon followed. But it wasn't until the twentieth century that children's Christmas music really took off with the recording of "Santa Claus Is Coming to Town," "Frosty the Snowman," and of course the song about everyone's favourite red-nosed reindeer.

Looking back, some of the best-known Christmas songs of the past seventy years have been written for children. As such, we felt that this book would have been incomplete without a section devoted to the genre of Rudolph and friends.

Brainteaser Trivia

(Answers on page 225)

Pumpkin Pies

1. In the song "Jolly Old St. Nicholas," how does the singer's stocking stand out from all the other stockings by the chimney?

   a. It's red

   b. It's striped

   c. It's the shortest

   d. It's covered in jingle bells

2. The popular Christmas song "Frosty the Snowman" was first recorded in 1950 by which famous singing cowboy?

   a. Roy Rogers

   b. Tex Ritter

   c. John Wayne

   d. Gene Autry

3. Which famous Christmas song was originally conceived as a poem that helped to cheer up a grieving little girl who'd recently lost her mother?

   a. "Rudolph the Red-Nosed Reindeer"

   b. "Frosty the Snowman"

   c. "The Chipmunk Song"

   d. "Suzy Snowflake"

4. How did Ross Bagdasarian, singer and songwriter of "The Chipmunk Song (Christmas Don't Be Late)," achieve the trademark high-pitched chipmunk voices on the 1958 holiday hit?

    a. He inhaled helium before singing
    b. He used a trio of talented five-year-olds
    c. He played back his own voice at high speed
    d. He taught real chipmunks how to sing

5. Name the holiday song that is essentially a list of naughty pranks perpetuated by a mischievous little boy.

    a. "Santa Claus Is Coming to Town"
    b. "Old Toy Trains"
    c. "Nuttin' for Christmas"
    d. "I Saw Mommy Kissing Santa Claus"

6. In the song "Rudolph the Red-Nosed Reindeer," what type of weather condition compelled Santa to ask Rudolph to guide his sleigh?

    a. Snow   b. Sleet   c. Rain   d. Fog

7. Elmo Shropshire is famous around the world for recording the holiday favourite "Grandma Got Run Over by a Reindeer." Aside from singing, what is his other profession?

    a. Veterinarian   c. Astronaut
    b. School bus driver   d. Trapeze artist

8. How old was Barry Gordon when he recorded the novelty song "Nuttin' for Christmas"?

   a. Six   b. Sixteen   c. Twenty-six   d. Thirty-six

9. Where is Santa Claus coming in Gene Autry's 1947 holiday favourite "Here Comes Santa Claus"?

   a. Down the chimney   c. Across the starry skies
   b. Down Santa Claus Lane   d. Straight for the milk and cookies

10. What was Frosty's nose made from in the holiday song "Frosty the Snowman"?

    a. A carrot   b. Coal   c. A button   d. A corncob

11. Which child's stocking is filled first in the Christmas classic "Up On the Housetop"?

    a. Little Nell   b. Little Will   c. Little Bill   d. Tiny Tim

12. Which famous children's entertainer recorded the holiday song "Must Be Santa" on his 1976 best-selling album *Singable Songs for the Very Young*?

    a. Fred Penner   c. Kermit the Frog
    b. Captain Kangaroo   d. Raffi

13. According to composer Albert Hague, what type of music inspired the song "Trim up the Tree" in the classic television special *How the Grinch Stole Christmas!*?

a. Waltz   b. Rap   c. Blues   d. Polka

14. Which famous cartoon voice actor recorded the Looney Tunes holiday song "I Tan't Wait Till Quithmuth Day"?

a. Mel Blanc   c. Casey Kasem
b. Hank Azaria   d. Tom Bosley

15. In the lyrics of the 1949 holiday song "A Marshmallow World," what kind of sweet treat is snow compared to?

a. Meringue   c. Vanilla fudge
b. Whipped cream   d. Icing sugar

16. Why does the singer of "All I Want for Christmas Is My Two Front Teeth" want the teeth?

a. To wish you Merry Christmas
b. To kiss mommy
c. To eat candy canes
d. To chew bubble gum

17. What time is it when Santa arrives in "Jolly Old St. Nicholas"?

a. One A.M.   c. Twelve o'clock
b. Half past midnight   d. A quarter to three

Plum Puddings

18. What gift does the "boy child" want for Christmas in the Johnny Marks song "Run Rudolph Run"?

    a. A bongo drum set
    b. A rock-and-roll electric guitar
    c. A synthesizer keyboard
    d. A stereo hi-fi

19. What was Donald Yetter Gardner's profession when he wrote the famous song "All I Want for Christmas Is My Two Front Teeth" in 1944?

    a. Boxer   b. Dentist   c. Teacher   d. Hockey player

20. Which children's Christmas song was written by celebrated American songwriter Roger Miller?

    a. "Rudolph the Red-Nosed Reindeer"
    b. "Old Toy Trains"
    c. "I Saw Mommy Kissing Santa Claus"
    d. "Marshmallow World"

21. How old was Gayla Peevey when she recorded the novelty song "I Want a Hippopotamus for Christmas" in 1953?

    a. Six   b. Eight   c. Ten   d. Twelve

22. Where did writer Haven Gillespie come up with the lyrics to the 1934 Christmas standard "Santa Claus Is Coming to Town"?

a. On a horse-drawn sled   c. On a bus

b. On a subway   d. On an airplane

23. What was Gene Autry doing when he was first inspired to write the famous holiday song "Here Comes Santa Claus"?

a. Putting presents under his Christmas tree

b. Riding in a Christmas parade

c. Eating milk and cookies

d. Growing his first beard

24. What happened to singers Elmo and Patsy one year after they recorded their holiday hit "Grandma Got Run Over by a Reindeer"?

a. They married

b. They were run over by a car

c. They won the lottery

d. They divorced

25. How old was Jimmy Boyd when he recorded the 1952 holiday hit "I Saw Mommy Kissing Santa Claus"?

a. Six   b. Eight   c. Ten   d. Twelve

26. Why did songwriter Randy Brooks offer up the rights to his soon-to-be hit song "Grandma Got Run Over by a Reindeer" to Elmo and Patsy?
    a. His band wouldn't let him record it
    b. He was retiring from the music industry
    c. His grandmother hated the song
    d. He no longer believed in Christmas

27. What is the holiday song "Thirty-Two Feet—Eight Little Tails" referring to?
    a. Santa's reindeer
    b. Snow rabbits
    c. Workshop elves
    d. Nativity sheep

28. Name the Christmas song "barked" in the famous 1955 holiday recording by The Singing Dogs.
    a. "Silent Night"
    b. "Little Drummer Boy"
    c. "Jingle Bells"
    d. "Let It Snow"

29. What does Little Will's stocking get filled with in the holiday favourite "Up on the Housetop"?
    a. An electric train and track
    b. A BB gun
    c. A hammer and lots of tacks
    d. Lego

30. What was the name of "The Little Fir Tree" that Gene Autry sang about in his 1953 holiday recording?
    a. Felix   b. Frank   c. Freddie   d. Finnegan

31. Which famous Christmas song composer set Clement C. Moore's poem *A Visit From St. Nicholas* to music with "The Night Before Christmas Song"?

a. Irving Berlin   c. Alfred Burt

b. Johnny Marks   d. Tchaikovsky

32. What is the French version of Roger Miller's "Old Toy Trains" called?

a. "Vieux jouets"   c. "Père Noël"

b. "Vive le vent"   d. "Petit garçon"

33. How old was Brenda Lee when she recorded her first Christmas single, "Christy Christmas"/"I'm Gonna Lasso Santa Claus"?

a. Seven   b. Nine   c. Eleven   d. Thirteen

Chestnuts

34. Which famous Christmas song starts out with the lyric: "I just came back from a lovely trip along the Milky Way"?

a. "Santa Claus Is Coming to Town"

b. "Rudolph the Red-Nosed Reindeer"

c. "Here Comes Santa Claus"

d. "Up on the Housetop"

35. According to the website www.antiqueweek.com, how much money could you expect to get for an original Columbia Record Label seventy-eight RPM of "Frosty the Snowman" or "Rudolph the Red-Nosed Reindeer" today?

    a. One dollar

    b. Ten dollars

    c. One hundred dollars

    d. One thousand dollars

36. Dr. Elmo Shropshire has recorded several novelty Christmas songs. Which of the following is *not* one of them?

    a. "Grandma Got Run Over by a Reindeer"

    b. "Grandpa's Gonna Sue the Pants Off of Santa"

    c. "Don't Make Me Play That Grandma Song Again"

    d. "Over the River and Through the Woods to Grandma's House We Go"

37. Name the 1960s group that wrote several songs based on Charles Schulz's comic strip dog, including the holiday tune "Snoopy's Christmas."

    a. The Dave Clark Five

    b. The Royal Guardsmen

    c. The Beatles

    d. The Monkees

38. Which famous American singer recorded the holiday song "Suzy Snowflake" in 1951?

    a. Rosemary Clooney

    b. Patsy Cline

    c. Ella Fitzgerald

    d. Judy Garland

39. In "The Littlest Snowman," a holiday song by Bob Keeshan (Captain Kangaroo), what was the title character's heart made of?

 a. Ice   b. Coal   c. Red candy   d. Tin

40. Along with the Easter song "Here Comes Peter Cottontail," which other famous holiday tune did writers Steve Nelson and Jack Rollins sell to Gene Autry back in 1950?

 a. "Santa Baby"
 b. "Jolly Old St. Nicholas"
 c. "Frosty the Snowman"
 d. "I Saw Mommy Kissing Santa Claus"

41. The song "Over the River and Through the Woods" was based on a poem written by Lydia Maria Child in 1844. Instead of "Grandmother's house," what was the sled's destination in the original version?

 a. Cousin Mary's house   c. Grandfather's house
 b. Uncle Sam's house   d. Santa Claus's house

42. Name the Christmas sequel to Bobby Pickett's 1962 Halloween hit "Monster Mash."

 a. "Calamity Claus"   c. "Graveyard Noël"
 b. "Horror Show Christmas"   d. "Monsters' Holiday"

43. What does Susy want in "Jolly Old St. Nicholas"?
    a. A sled
    b. A picture book
    c. A pair of skates
    d. Christmas shoes

44. Name the Chipmunk imitation band that released the holiday song "Please Don't Take My Tree for Christmas."
    a. The Heavy Hamsters
    b. The Nutty Squirrels
    c. The Groovy Gerbils
    d. The Wicked Woodchucks

45. Barry Gordon, the singer of the famous song "Nuttin' for Christmas," was also the voice of which famous commercial cartoon character?
    a. Tony the Tiger
    b. The Nestlé Quik Bunny
    c. The Pillsbury Doughboy
    d. Snap (from Rice Krispies)

46. Which children's holiday song appeared on the flip side of Rosemary Clooney's 1951 recording of "Suzy Snowflake"?
    a. "Little Red Riding Hood's Christmas Tree"
    b. "The Three Little Pigs Visit Santa Claus"
    c. "Snow White and the Christmas Stocking"
    d. "Little Bo Peep's Snowy Holiday"

47. Which of the following artists was the first to record his version of "Santa Claus Is Coming to Town" back in 1935?

a. Tommy Dorsey

c. Nat King Cole

b. Gene Autry

d. Bing Crosby

48. The song "I Want a Hippopotamus for Christmas" helped raise money to acquire a hippo for which city's hippo-less zoo?

a. New York City

c. Salt Lake City

b. Oklahoma City

d. Kansas City

49. "Petit Papa Noël" is a children's Christmas song originally from which French-speaking country?

a. Canada   b. Belgium   c. Switzerland   d. France

50. What child singer performed the song "Got a Cold in the Node for Christmas" for the Columbia Records label?

a. Brenda Lee

c. Gayla Peevey

b. Shirley Temple

d. Jimmy Boyd

51. Who made the first recording of "All I Want for Christmas Is My Two Front Teeth"?

a. Perry Como

c. The Chipmunks

b. Gene Autry

d. Spike Jones

52. Which of the following was *not* recorded by Spike Jones and his City Slickers?

    a. *The Nutcracker*
    b. "All I Want for Christmas Is My Two Front Teeth"
    c. "I Want Eddie Fisher for Christmas"
    d. "Rudolph the Red-Nosed Reindeer"

Did You Know?

You'd Better Watch Out!

Can you name the Christmas song that has prompted millions of children around the world to keep their naughty impulses in check during the holiday season?

A song that nobody wanted to record because it wasn't commercial enough?

A song that has since gone on to become one of the most popular holiday songs in history (outsold only by "White Christmas" and "Rudolph the Red-Nosed Reindeer")?

Of course, that song is "Santa Claus Is Coming to Town," written by Haven Gillespie and Fred Coots in 1932.

The lyrics came easily for Gillespie, who, according to one story, wrote them during a fifteen-minute train ride to New York City.

Getting the song published, however, proved to be much trickier. It was a pretty hard sell back in those Great Depression-era days. "Kiddie" Christmas songs weren't a very big business back then. For two years it was rejected time and time again until comedian Eddie Cantor finally agreed to try it out on his Thanksgiving radio show— only at his wife Ida's insistence.

The song was an overnight sensation. According to Wikipedia, four hundred thousand copies of the sheet music were sold by Christmas of that same year. And the rest, as they say, is history.

Almost seventy-five years later, the song that nobody wanted has now been recorded by everyone from Bing Crosby to Bruce Springsteen to the Beach Boys and has even inspired its own animated television special (1970's *Santa Claus Is Coming to Town*).

But perhaps most importantly, it changed the face of Christmas music as we know it, opening the door for other "kiddie" holiday hits to come. One can't help wondering where Rudolph, Frosty, and even the Grinch would be today if Santa Claus *hadn't* come to town.

"Rudolph the Red-Nosed Reindeer"

Despite what your average five-year-old might think, Santa Claus didn't *always* have nine reindeer pulling his sleigh. In fact, it wasn't until 1939 that Rudolph joined the team of Dasher, Dancer, Prancer, Vixen, Comet, Cupid, Donner, and Blitzen.

The celebrated reindeer was created by thirty-four-year-old copywriter Robert May as a promotional character for his employer, Chicago-based department store chain Montgomery Ward.

May, whose wife was terminally ill at the time, based the character of the ostracized red-nosed reindeer on his own experiences as a misfit child. He asked Denver Gillen, a colleague from Montgomery Ward's art department, to go with him to the Lincoln Park Zoo to sketch some deer for the illustrations. In search of an alliterative *R* moniker for his creation, May tried out *Rollo* and *Reginald* before his four-year-old daughter Barbara helped him settle on the name *Rudolph*.

The story was a hit with the kids and Montgomery Ward distributed millions of free copies of its Rudolph booklets between 1939 and 1946. In 1947, the department store kindly transferred the copyright for Rudolph over to May, who was still deeply in debt from his late wife's medical bills.

Soon after, May's brother-in-law (songwriter Johnny Marks) set the story of the red-nosed reindeer to music and began the search for someone to record it. After it was turned down by several big-name stars, Gene Autry reluctantly agreed to do it after being persuaded by his wife.

In 1949, "Rudolph the Red-Nosed Reindeer" was released and quickly became a phenomenon, selling two million copies in that first year alone. It went on to become one of the world's most popular holiday songs, outsold only by "White Christmas."

But perhaps more importantly, Robert May's little misfit reindeer accomplished what no one has been able to since—he significantly altered the accepted legend of Santa Claus. And because of this, he will certainly go down in history.

A Hippopotamus for Christmas?

What little kid doesn't dream of getting a new pet for Christmas? Most children wish for something like a puppy, a kitten, a bunny rabbit, or even a goldfish. Well, in 1953, little Gayla Peevey got something a bit bigger, and certainly more exotic.

At just ten years old, Peevey was a budding child star with her recording of the novelty song "I Want a Hippopotamus for Christmas." It was an instant hit.

Coincidentally, the same year the song came out, the zoo in Gayla's hometown of Oklahoma City was in need of a hippo. Her song sparked the idea for a fundraising campaign to "buy Gayla a hippo for Christmas" (contrary to urban legend, the song was not recorded expressly for this purpose).

Kids around the city pitched in—eagerly opening their piggy banks and sending in their pennies until soon enough the zoo had raised three thousand dollars, which was enough money (back in those days) to buy a baby hippo.

After being presented with her new pet hippopotamus, Matilda, Gayla promptly donated her right back to the Oklahoma City Zoo, where the hippo lived happily until her passing in March 1998.

Peevey went on to record other children's songs, such as "Got a Cold in the Node for Christmas" and "Angel in the Christmas Play."

Just Hear Those Ice Cubes Jingling

In 1946, Singing Cowboy Gene Autry was riding his horse Champion in the annual Hollywood Christmas Parade when he was inspired to write one of the world's most commercially successful holiday songs.

Heading down Hollywood Boulevard ahead of Santa's float, Autry heard the excited voices of children calling, "Here comes Santa Claus!"

The idea for a hit song was born right then and there.

Autry sketched out "Here Comes Santa Claus" on paper and handed his notes over to a couple of his musical colleagues, Oakley Haldeman and Uncle Art Satherley.

According to liner notes written by Jon Guyot Smith from the box set *Sing, Cowboy, Sing!: The Gene Autry Collection* (Rhino Records, 1997), something interesting happened during the recording of the demo tape at the home of singer Johnny Bond:

"A cocktail was mixed for Uncle Art, who sipped near the microphone while Bond sang *Here Comes Santa Claus* for the first time. When the group heard the ice cubes jingling so merrily on the playback, they were inspired to use a 'jingle bell' sound on Gene's record!"

Cocktails and St. Nick made for a profitable combination. Autry's recording became a success, selling over two million copies and hitting the pop charts several times in the following years.

And today, sixty years after that original Christmas parade, "Here Comes Santa Claus" is still popular. The Elvis Presley recording of the song was ranked number twenty-one on the American Society of

Composers, Authors and Publishers (ASCAP) list of top twenty-five holiday songs in 2006.

Gordon Pape Reminisces About Spike Jones

Memory is a strange thing. Now that I'm in my seventies, I find that I occasionally can't remember what I'm looking for when I walk into a room. But I can recall virtually all the lyrics from a record album I first heard more than sixty years ago, when I was nine years old: Spike Jones's irreverent version of *The Nutcracker.*

Most people born after 1965 have probably never heard of Spike Jones, who died that year at the age of fifty-three. But kids who grew up during the years of the Second World War loved his zany send-ups of popular and classical music, which came complete with honking horns, cowbells, gunshots, braying donkeys, weird laughter, creaking doors, and just about every other sound effect you can imagine.

My introduction to classical music was listening to Jones and his City Slickers do their take-off on the "William Tell Overture" (Rossini), "Liebesträume" (Liszt), "Dance of the Hours" (Ponchielli), and many more. I never tired of hearing his comic tributes to popular songs of the day, such as "Cocktails for Two," "Laura," "Glow Worm," and "I'm in the Mood for Love."

But it was his "Nutcracker Suite" that I loved most of all. I can still remember opening the gift on Christmas morning, 1945. The album cover was colourfully decorated with characters from the ballet and across the bottom was emblazoned: "With apologies to Tchaikovsky." Inside were two seventy-eight RPM vinyl records. I couldn't wait to listen to it on our old Victrola.

From the very first words—"Once, on a Christmas Eve a little girl lay dreaming"—I was hooked. I spent hours during that holiday season listening as Jones and his crazy crew told the story of the magical Nutcracker, the Mouse King and his army, the Sugar Plum Fairy, the waltzing flowers, and the Land of the Lemon Drops.

I realize that today parts of the suite, such as the dance of the Chinese dolls, might be deemed offensive by some. But back in those days, with the war still fresh in everyone's minds, it was all just good fun. And for a kid of nine, growing up in the pre-television era, Jones provided a magical trip to the ultimate fantasy land.

To this day, I can sing (poorly, I admit) every word from that album, as I proved to my daughter Deborah and her family at our 2006 Christmas Day celebration. That's how deep an impact it made.

I kept that album for years, but when I tried to find it to play for my grandchildren it had disappeared—lost in one of our many family moves. So I was delighted when Deborah downloaded it onto a CD from iTunes (www.apple.com/itunes) and presented it to me as a gift.

I'll listen to it again, although I don't really need to. It's all up there in my head. Maybe that's why I can't remember why I walked into this room!

Answers

The Earliest Carols

Pumpkin Pies (one point each)

1. b.	4. b.	7. c.	10. c.
2. d.	5. d.	8. b.	
3. a.	6. d.	9. c.	

Plum Puddings (two points each)

11. b.	14. c.	17. b.	20. d.
12. a.	15. b.	18. b.	21. a.
13. b.	16. a.	19. c.	

Chestnuts (three points each)

22. b.	26. c.	30. c.	34. a.
23. b.	27. a.	31. c.	35. b.
24. b.	28. a.	32. a.	36. c.
25. a.	29. b.	33. c.	

English Carols

Pumpkin Pies (one point each)

1. a.	6. c.	11. c.	16. a.
2. c.	7. b.	12. c.	17. b.
3. b.	8. c.	13. d.	18. d.
4. c.	9. b.	14. d.	19. a.
5. c.	10. b.	15. d.	20. a.

Plum Puddings (two points each)

21. c.	26. b.	31. a.	36. d.
22. b.	27. d.	32. d.	37. b.
23. a.	28. c.	33. a.	38. d.
24. c.	29. c.	34. a.	39. d.
25. d.	30. c.	35. b.	40. d.

Chestnuts (three points each)

41. a.	47. c.	53. d.	59. b.
42. c.	48. d.	54. b.	60. a.
43. c.	49. d.	55. d.	61. c.
44. c.	50. b.	56. b.	
45. a.	51. b.	57. a.	
46. b.	52. d.	58. d.	

Franco/Germanic Carols

Pumpkin Pies (one point each)

1. c.	5. b.	9. d.	13. a.
2. b.	6. c.	10. b.	14. c.
3. a.	7. b.	11. d.	15. b.
4. b.	8. c.	12. d.	

Plum Puddings (two points each)

16. b.	21. b.	26. c.	31. c.
17. a.	22. b.	27. d.	32. a.
18. a.	23. a.	28. a.	33. c.
19. b.	24. c.	29. c.	
20. c.	25. a.	30. c.	

Chestnuts (three points each)

34. b.	40. c.	46. d.	52. c.
35. a., b.	41. d.	47. d.	53. b.
36. b.	42. a.	48. d.	54. c.
37. c.	43. d.	49. b.	
38. a.	44. d.	50. a.	
39. b.	45. a.	51. b.	

American Carols

Pumpkin Pies (one point each)

1. b.	6. b.	11. a.	16. b.
2. a.	7. c.	12. b.	17. c.
3. d.	8. a.	13. a.	18. d.
4. b.	9. b.	14. c.	
5. b.	10. c.	15. b.	

Plum Puddings (two points each)

19. b.	24. b.	29. c.	34. b.
20. c.	25. c.	30. b.	35. c.
21. a.	26. a.	31. a.	36. b.
22. b.	27. b.	32. d.	
23. b.	28. c.	33. a.	

Chestnuts (three points each)

37. b.	42. b.	47. c.	52. b.
38. c.	43. c.	48. d.	53. a.
39. d.	44. b.	49. a.	54. d.
40. b.	45. c.	50. d.	55. c.
41. c.	46. a.	51. a.	

Carols from Around the World

Pumpkin Pies (one point each)

1. a.	7. a.	13. a.	19. c.
2. d.	8. a.	14. a.	20. d.
3. a.	9. b.	15. a.	21. c.
4. b.	10. c.	16. d.	22. a.
5. b.	11. c.	17. c.	23. d.
6. b.	12. a.	18. b.	24. c.

Plum Puddings (two points each)

25. d.	31. c.	37. a.	43. b.
26. c.	32. b.	38. d.	44. c.
27. c.	33. c.	39. b.	45. d.
28. d.	34. a.	40. c.	46. a.
29. a.	35. c.	41. d.	47. c.
30. c.	36. a.	42. c.	

Chestnuts (three points each)

48. c.	54. c.	60. c.	66. c.
49. a.	55. c.	61. b.	67. a.
50. b.	56. b.	62. c.	68. d.
51. b.	57. d.	63. c.	69. a.
52. d.	58. d.	64. b.	70. b.
53. d.	59. b.	65. c.	71. c.

Classical Carols

Pumpkin Pies (one point each)

1. c.	4. c.	7. d.	10. c.
2. b.	5. d.	8. b.	11. a.
3. d.	6. c.	9. c.	

Plum Puddings (two points each)

12. d	16. b.	20. b.	24. b.
13. d.	17. c.	21. c.	
14. a.	18. a.	22. c.	
15. c.	19. b.	23. a.	

Chestnuts (three points each)

25. d.	30. d.	35. b.	40. d.
26. d.	31. a.	36. b.	41. d.
27. b.	32. c.	37. d.	42. d.
28. b.	33. a.	38. d.	43. c.
29. d.	34. b.	39. b.	

Modern Carols

Pumpkin Pies (one point each)

1. d.	7. d.	13. b.	19. a.
2. c.	8. c.	14. b.	20. b.
3. d.	9. b.	15. d.	21. c.
4. b.	10. d.	16. a.	22. d.
5. d.	11. c.	17. b.	23. a.
6. d.	12. c.	18. c.	24. b.

Plum Puddings (two points each)

25. c.	32. d.	39. a.	46. b.
26. b.	33. d.	40. a.	47. d.
27. c.	34. a.	41. c.	48. a.
28. d.	35. d.	42. b.	49. d.
29. a.	36. b.	43. c.	50. c.
30. d.	37. a.	44. d.	
31. a.	38. a.	45. c.	

Chestnuts (three points each)

51. b.	57. a.	63. c.	69. d.
52. d.	58. a.	64. b.	70. b.
53. d.	59. a.	65. c.	71. c.
54. c.	60. a.	66. a.	72. a.
55. a.	61. b.	67. a.	73. c.
56. a.	62. a.	68. b.	

Carols on Stage, Screen, Radio, and TV

Pumpkin Pies (one point each)

1. b.	6. c.	11. d.	16. d.
2. c.	7. a.	12. c.	17. c.
3. b.	8. a.	13. c.	18. d.
4. c.	9. c.	14. a.	19. d.
5. c.	10. a.	15. a.	20. c.

Plum Puddings (two points each)

21. b.	26. b.	31. a.	36. a.
22. d.	27. d.	32. c.	37. b.
23. d.	28. c.	33. d.	38. a.
24. a.	29. d.	34. c.	39. c.
25. b.	30. d.	35. d.	40. b.

Chestnuts (three points each)

41. c.	47. b.	53. a.	59. a.
42. b.	48. b.	54. b.	60. b.
43. b.	49. c.	55. b.	61. b.
44. c.	50. c.	56. d.	62. c.
45. a.	51. a.	57. b.	
46. b.	52. a.	58. a.	

Children's Christmas Songs

Pumpkin Pies (one point each)

1. c.	6. d.	11. a.	16. a.
2. d.	7. a.	12. d.	17. c.
3. a.	8. a.	13. d.	
4. c.	9. b.	14. a.	
5. c.	10. c.	15. b.	

Plum Puddings (two points each)

18. b.	22. b.	26. a.	30. c.
19. c.	23. b.	27. a.	31. b.
20. b.	24. d.	28. c.	32. d.
21. c.	25. d.	29. c.	33. c.

Chestnuts (three points each)

34. a.	39. c.	44. b.	49. d.
35. b.	40. c.	45. b.	50. c.
36. d.	41. c.	46. a.	51. d.
37. b.	42. d.	47. a.	52. d.
38. a.	43. a.	48. b.	

Selected Readings

*H*ere are the books and websites we used in researching this book. We recommend them as excellent resources for readers who would like more information about the rich history of Christmas carols.

BOOKS

Ayres, Anne. *The Life and Work of William Augustus Muhlenberg.* New York: T. Whittaker, 1889. Available as an e-book from Project Canterbury http://anglicanhistory.org/usa/muhlenberg/ayres/20.html.

Bowler, Gerry. *The World Encyclopedia of Christmas.* Toronto, ON: McClelland & Stewart Ltd., 2000.

Brooks, Phillips. *Addresses.* Philadelphia, PA: Henry Altemus, 1895. Available as an e-book from Project Gutenberg www.gutenberg.org.

Collins, Ace. *Stories Behind the Best-Loved Songs of Christmas.* Grand Rapids, MI: Zondervan, 2001.

Collins, Ace. *More Stories Behind the Best-Loved Songs of Christmas.* Grand Rapids, MI: Zondervan, 2006.

Cousin, John W. *A Short Biographical Dictionary of English Literature.* London: J.M. Dent & Sons, 1910. Available as an e-book from Project Gutenberg www.gutenberg.org.

Crump, William D. *The Christmas Encyclopedia.* Jefferson, NC: McFarland & Company, Inc., Publishers, 2001.

Keyte, Hugh, and Andrew Parrott, editors. *The New Oxford Book of Carols.* Oxford: Oxford University Press, 1992.

Menendez, Albert J., and Shirley C. Menendez. *Christmas Songs Made in America.* Nashville, TN: Cumberland House, 1999.

Menendez, Albert J., and Shirley C. Menendez. *Joy to the World.* Nashville, TN: Cumberland House, 2001.

Nobbman, Dale V. *Christmas Music Companion Fact Book.* Anaheim Hills, CA: Centerstream Publishing, 2000.

Reynolds, Virginia. *The Spirit of Christmas.* White Plains, NY: Peter Pauper Press, Inc., 2000.

Studwell, William. *The Christmas Carol Reader.* Binghamton, NY: Harrington Park Press, 1995.

Websites

Abraham Lincoln's Assassination
http://members.aol.com/RVSNorton/Lincoln.html

Alexander, Mrs. Cecil Frances ("Once in Royal David's City") http://find articles.com/p/articles/mi_qa3724/is_200308/ai_n9252765

Antique Week www.antiqueweek.com

Arthritis Foundation www.arthritis.org

Australian Carols www.cultureandrecreation.gov.au/articles/christmas/

Autry, Gene www.geneautry.com/clubhouse/christmas/christmassongs.html

Berlioz, Hector www.hberlioz.com/Scores/senfance.htm

Boar's Head Carol http://ancienthistory.about.com/od/music/a/BoarsHead.htm, www.queens.ox.ac.uk, http://mymerrychristmas.com/2005/boar.shtml

BrainyQuote.com www.brainyquote.com

Britten, Benjamin www.its.caltech.edu/~tan/Britten, www.brittenpears.org,
     www.karadar.com/Dictionary/britten.html

Burt, Alfred www.alfredburtcarols.com/

Carols www.carols.org

Catholic Encyclopedia www.newadvent.org

Ceremony of Carols www.napervillechorus.org/ceremony.html,
     www.bostoncecilia.org/prognotes/britten-ceremony.html,
     www.everything2.com/index.pl?node=Ceremony%20of%20Carols

"Christmas Shoes" www.theydeserveit.com/christmas/shoes-song.html,
     www.findarticles.com/p/articles/mi_m1058/is_2_120/ai_97173985,
     www.julicragghilliard.com/work47.htm,
     www.ntu.edu.sg/home/hblim/passages/goldenshoes.htm,
     http://annekenstein.typepad.com/monster/2004/11/the_christmas_s.html

Cyber Hymnal www.cyberhymnal.org

Earliest Carols
     www.hymnsandcarolsofchristmas.com/Hymns_and_Carols/Images/
     Rickert/ancient_english_christmas_carols_intro.htm,
     www.1911encyclopedia.org/Carol

Encyclopedia Brittanica Online www.britannica.com

English Carols www.sacred-texts.com/neu/celt/fim/fim09.htm

French Christmas Carols
     http://french.about.com/od/christmascarols/French_Christmas_Carols_
     Chants_de_Nol.htm

General Carol Trivia www.lewrockwell.com/north/north333.html,
     www.mistletunes.com/index.html, http://arts.guardian.co.uk/christmas
     2003/story/0,,1100170,00.html, www.phillyburbs.com/christmascarols/,
     www.startribune.com/389/story/63313.html,
     http://en.wikipedia.org/wiki/Christmas_song

Google www.google.com

"Hallelujah Chorus" www.festival-singers.org.nz/haleluia.htm,
    www.hallelujah-chorus.com
Handel, George Frideric www2.nau.edu/~tas3/handel.html,
    www.baroquemusic.org/bqxhandel.html
History of Carols www.whychristmas.com/customs/carols_history.shtml,
    www.christianitytoday.com/history/newsletter/christmas/carol.html,
    http://christmas.howstuffworks.com/christmas-songs33.htm
The Huron Carol www.culture.gouv.fr/culture/noel/angl/amerind.htm,
    www.rivernen.ca/legend_6.htm
Hymns and Carols of Christmas www.hymnsandcarolsofchristmas.com
"I Saw Three Ships" www.hymnsandcarolsofchristmas.com/Hymns_and_
    Carols/i_saw_three_ships.htm
Index of All Carols www.hymnsandcarolsofchristmas.com/HTML/full_
    index_of_hymns_and_carols.htm
Irish Carols www.of-ireland.info/holidays/carols.html,
    www.irishcultureandcustoms.com/ACalend/XmasDingDong.html
Jones, Spike www.spikejones.net,
    www.pynchon.pomona.edu/uncollected/spiked.html
"Merry Christmas, Darling" www.richardandkarencarpenter.com/Album_
    ChristmasCollection.htm
National Public Radio www.npr.org
Negro Spirituals www.negrospirituals.com
New Zealand Carols http://folksong.org.nz/nzchristmas/index.html
Niles, John Jacob www.john-jacob-niles.com
"O Holy Night" http://home.att.net/~yorkrose02/oholynight.html,
    www.culture.gouv.fr/culture/noel/franc/chan-mc.htm,
    www.uua.org/uuhs/duub/articles/johnsullivandwight.html,
    www.hymnsandcarolsofchristmas.com/Hymns_and_Carols/o_holy_
    night.htm
Papers of Phillips Brooks and the Brooks Family, Harvard University Library,

Online Archival Search Information System
http://oasis.harvard.edu:10080/oasis/deliver/~hou00459
Project Gutenberg Literary Archive Foundation www.gutenberg.org
"Rudolph the Red-Nosed Reindeer"
www.snopes.com/holidays/christmas/rudolph.asp
Schubert, Franz http://home.swipnet.se/~w-18046/schub.html,
www.classicalarchives.com/bios/codm/schubert.html,
www.franzschubert.org.uk/intro/index.html
Seuse, Heinrich www.nndb.com/people/316/000098022/,
www.britannica.com/ebc/article-9070491,
www.newadvent.org/cathen/07238c.htm
"Silent Night" www.silentnightmuseum.org
"Silver Bells" www.npr.org/templates/story/story.php?storyId=5068947
Singing Dogs www.bobshannon.com/specials/dogs.html
Slovakian Carols www.iarelative.com/xmas/
"The Snow Lay on the Ground"
http://books.google.com/books?id=rhL8kHK48ycC&pg=PA49&lpg=
PA49&dq=19th+century+the+snow+lay+on+the+ground&source=
web&ots=cF_uoxnap2&sig=e0N0q9CSZaS4w6Qw-6Jh5J2YvGw
Spanish Carols www.escuelai.com/spanish_magazine/christmas_carols.html
Strauss, Richard www.richard-strauss.com,
w3.rz-berlin.mpg.de/cmp/strauss_r.html,
www.richardstrauss.at/html_e/17_willkommen/0fs_index.html,
www.classicalarchives.com/bios/codm/strauss.html
Tate, Nahum www.litencyc.com/php/speople.php?rec=true&UID=4317,
www.nndb.com/people/448/000098154
Twelve Days of Christmas, www.crivoice.org/cy12days.html
Unusual Christmas Carols, http://tcpiii.tripod.com/christmascarols.htm
"A Virgin Unspotted" www.cyberhymnal.org/htm/v/i/r/virginus.htm

"White Christmas" www.simonsays.com/content/book.cfm?isbn=
     0743218752&sid=33&agid=2
Wikipedia, The Free Encyclopedia www.wikipedia.org
"The Yankee Tunesmiths" Amaranth Publishing
     www.amaranthpublishing.com/billings.htm

NEWSPAPERS AND PERIODICALS

Atlantic Monthly. Boston MA: Atlantic Monthly Company.
Globe and Mail, The. Toronto ON: Bell Globemedia Publishing
Phillips Brooks by Alexander V.G. Allen, published April 1893, available
     online through Cornell University Library
     http://cdl.library.cornell.edu/cgi-bin/moa/sgml/moa-idx?notisid=
     ABK2934-0071-73
Toronto Star, The. Toronto ON: Torstar Corp.

Acknowledgments

*T*he history of carols is as old as the Christian church and as new as the next pop Christmas song to be released. Classic carols are reverent and often solemn, but Christmas music today is more frequently secular, frequently nostalgic, and sometimes intentionally funny.

Creating a book of trivia and stories based on Christmas carols therefore involved researching a broad range of music, from monastic chants to hip-hop. To do that, we drew on a wide range of sources, both print and electronic. In some cases, the two were combined in obscure literary works that have been made accessible in the form of e-books through initiatives such as Project Gutenberg and Project Canterbury. We would like to acknowledge the tremendously valuable work being done by such foundations in preserving writings that might otherwise have been lost to all but the most dedicated scholars.

In Selected Readings, you will find a list of the many sources we consulted. We want to acknowledge our debt of gratitude to the creators of all these works, but most particularly to Hugh Keyte and Andrew Parrott, editors of *The New Oxford Book of Carols,* which is the seminal reference source for anyone interested in the history of carols.

We also want to thank all of our editors, without whose tireless efforts books like this would not exist. They include senior editors Andrea Magyar in Toronto and David Cashion in New York; our production editor, Sandra Tooze; our copy editor, Laurel Sparrow; and Ron Lightburn, who drew the cover illustration.